Honeybee Cottage

K.T. DADY

Honeybee Cottage
K.T. Dady

Sing a song that fills your heart.

1

Josh

Ever since he was a child, the safest place in the world to Josh Reynolds was his grandmother's bed. Whenever the night petrified him, he would tiptoe into her bedroom and gently tap her on the arm. One sleepy eye would peep up at him, and then the cover would be pulled back for him to slip into her bed, snuggle in her arms, and fall straight asleep. All his demons would immediately vanish, and he would sleep soundly.

Josh stared down at the double bed in front of him. It was half past three in the morning, the bed was empty, and it had been many years since his grandmother had helped him sleep.

At thirty-two years old, he still had trouble sleeping alone. He hated the dark and the night terrors that came with it.

His grandmother died three years ago, and his grandfather more recently. He had been raised by his grandparents ever since his parents died in a car accident when he was ten years old. Now all he had left of his family was his older brother, Jake.

Josh lowered his suitcase to the floor and stripped off down to his black boxer shorts. His clothes were wet from the torrential rain outside, so he flung them over the back of the light-wood rocking chair that was in the corner of the room. He sighed deeply, then pulled back the cream duvet and climbed into his gran's old bed.

The tea shop below his room made creaking noises that kept his eyes wide open. He stared over at the dark sky outside the small sash window.

A shiver ran the length of his spine, causing him to snuggle further into the bedding. He wanted the warmth of pyjamas, but he knew better than to wear any. Most nights he'd wake dripping in sweat, so he soon learned not to bother with nightclothes.

He tried to imagine that it was daytime and that his grandmother's tea shop below, Edith's Tearoom, was awash with customers. The smell of freshly baked cakes floated up to the flat above the shop, entering his room, warming his heart.

Christmas Eve tomorrow.

The memories from his childhood hit him hard. There were no more stockings hanging from the fireplace, no more cookies to decorate, no more festive cheer, no more laughter.

A lone tear rolled down the side of his face and sank into the pillow.

He felt so tired. His eyes were bloodshot, his body fatigued, and his soul numb.

His journey to his grandmother's childhood home in Pepper Bay had been long. He had travelled from New York to London, then from London to the Isle of Wight. He had paid an old friend to get out of bed in the wee small hours of the morning and use a fishing boat to transport him from Southampton to the island. The crossing over the water had been turbulent, making him feel sick.

He got out of bed and opened the window a few inches so that he could listen to the rain. He always enjoyed the sound of the rain, when he wasn't outside in it getting soaked. A cool, damp breeze blew gently through the gap. He inhaled the salty air and then swiftly returned to bed.

Come on, Josh, try and get some sleep. You know what to do. Breathe. Short breaths in, long breaths out. You're lying on the sand. The calm water is gently lapping at your feet. The sun is warm and soothing. Inhale. Exhale. I'm here. I'm on the beach. I'm relaxed. I'm in my grandmother's flat. I'm in Pepper Bay. It's the middle of the night. I am so not relaxed.

His eyes popped open to stare at the ceiling.

'This is your fault, Jake,' he whispered to the room.

What am I doing? Why did I come back? Why do I always come back here? You know why.

He took a deep breath and closed his eyes. Sooner or later, he would fall asleep. He just had to give in to the night.

He kept his eyes closed and his breathing steady, but he could feel his mind pulling him back every time his body attempted to give in to exhaustion.

A noise came from the living room, causing a thump to his heart.

What was that?

He opened his eyes and listened carefully, trying to figure out if it was the cracking sound of the fridge in the small kitchen or maybe the creaks of the old, quaint, pastel-pink shop in Pepper Lane.

A muffled clattering sound made him jump out of bed. His heart raced up towards his throat. Someone was outside, and there was no way he was about to let them take any of his grandmother's things.

Without thinking, he grabbed the floral bedside lamp, silently pulled the plug from the wall, held the round base up to his shoulder, and sneaked out to the living room.

A scream scared the living daylights out of him.

'Christ, Joey!'

He looked down to see Joey sitting on the floor in front of an opened cupboard in the kitchen, holding a metal mixing bowl on her lap and another one in her right hand.

She worked downstairs in Edith's Tearoom as a baker. She pretty much ran the place and had done so ever since Edith Reynolds had taught her everything she knew and put her in charge of her tea shop many years ago.

Joey's startled eyes stared up at him, then down at his boxers.

Josh lowered the lamp to his side as he caught his breath. 'I almost whacked you, Jo. What are you doing up here? It's not even four in the morning yet.'

He watched her swallow hard as she rolled her taupe eyes across his toned chest. He raised his eyebrows at her in tired amusement. He knew what was going through her mind.

Not now, Jo.

'It's Christmas Eve tomorrow,' she replied. Her voice was quiet and husky. 'I've got lots to do today. We have a tour coming in from Hotel Royale tomorrow morning.'

He carefully placed the lamp down on the small kitchen table behind him, trying not to scratch the already-scratched pine.

Her eyes were now fixed on his. 'What are you doing here?'

'Jake asked me to come for Christmas.'

'So why aren't you up at Starlight Cottage with him?'

He dropped his shoulders. 'I'm tired, Jo. I've not long got in. Wes Morland dropped me off down at the beach. I didn't have the energy to walk up to the top of Pepper Lane in this downpour. I'll go up there tomorrow. Well, later today, that is.'

She stood up and took a step closer towards him. 'It hasn't stopped raining the last couple of weeks. First we have a ton of snow land on us, and now this.'

Josh felt a flutter in his stomach appear. It was the same feeling he got whenever she was near him. It had been three years since he last looked in her eyes, but those three years suddenly felt like yesterday.

Her voice was soft and gentle as she asked, 'Have you been trying to sleep?'

He gave a half-shrug. He felt slightly embarrassed that she knew about his night troubles, but at the same time, he knew he could talk to her about anything and feel safe with her holding his secrets. She had always been his best friend, since they were teenagers. He shared so much of himself with her.

Joey reached out and touched his arm, sending a shiver of delight straight through him. She frowned with concern at his goosebumps. 'You're cold, Josh. Get back in bed. I'll help you sleep.'

He lowered his weary head and walked back into the bedroom. He could sense her walking behind him. Just her presence alone relaxed his soul. He climbed back into bed and watched her remove her slippers, brown jumper, and dark jeans. She was wearing plain black underwear that blended with the darkness of the room, causing her pale skin to appear ghostly. Her golden-blonde hair rolled down to sit upon her shoulders as she removed her hairband.

You're so beautiful, Jo.

Joey got into bed and pulled him closer to her warm body. 'Sleep now, Josh,' she whispered.

His head rested on her collarbone whilst his hand met her stomach where he gently stroked her skin with his thumb.

I've missed you, Joey Walker.

9

He took a calming breath as her fingers swept lightly through his short dark hair. He smiled softly, inhaling her sweet scent. He always thought she smelled like lemon cake. Her familiar citrus fragrance immediately warmed his heart. He relaxed into her soothing presence and closed his eyes.

2

Joey

It had been three years since Joey last saw Josh. He had stayed in Pepper Bay just for Edith's funeral and then left. It was the only time since they were seventeen that he had visited and they hadn't slept together during his stay.

Joey loved Josh with every fibre of her being, but she just couldn't take any more of him coming and going in her life. It wasn't his fault. He didn't know she loved him. He only came and went because he didn't live there.

Josh's grandmother had brought him to her family home, Starlight Cottage, every summer and sometimes at Christmas, and Joey had never given him any reason to stay longer. She was the one who treated him like a holiday fling. She took full responsibility for her actions. She had always been the instigator, right back from their first kiss to the day they lost their virginity to each other.

Josh was sound asleep. His breathing steady and relaxed.

She knew she would only have to hold him for five minutes for him to fall deeply into a calm sleep. She just wished he would fall deeply in love with her.

She had decided three years ago that she would get over her love for Josh Reynolds. She needed to move on and maybe one day she would be able to find a man who loved her back, get married, and have children, as that's what she wanted for her life. She had lived with the pain of heartache for too long.

I'm not breaking my rule. This is different. He needed me. I'm just helping him sleep.

She held off from stroking his thick dark hair again. Their close proximity was hard enough without her caressing him. *Five more minutes.*

He was already in a deep sleep, so she could now leave, but she wanted those extra five minutes just for herself.

Just a few more minutes of his body pressed against mine. He feels so good. I want to get closer to him. I have to stop thinking this way. Why is it so hard to stop loving him?

She closed her eyes for a moment and willingly entered her daydream.

These were the moments with him where she would pretend they were happily married and everything was perfect. He didn't sleep with other women. That life didn't exist. She was his one and only, and he loved her with all of his heart. He wasn't a millionaire coffee shop owner from London. He was simply Josh Reynolds, who loved living in Pepper Bay. Edith's Tearoom was their business, and their family was their life. They lived in Honeybee Cottage, her favourite out of all the cottages along Pepper Lane, and every night he would come home to her, and they would make love and fall asleep in each other's arms.

Tears welled in her eyes, bringing her back to reality. Her heart was breaking already.

Don't dream. Don't think. Go back to work.

She carefully removed herself from underneath Josh to slip out of the warmth of the bed. The breeze from the opened window caused her to shiver whilst she quickly got dressed.

The mixing bowls she had come for were still sitting on the kitchen floor. She picked them up and headed downstairs to the tea shop, quietly closing every door she left behind.

A gentle tapping noise hit the back door of the shop. Joey opened it to see Ruby Morland standing outside on the cobbles of the alleyway.

Ruby rubbed her arms along her dark-red coat. 'Ooh, let's get in, Jo. I'm cold.'

Joey closed the door as Ruby headed for the coat hooks to hang up her coat, hat, scarf, and umbrella.

'I've just put the heating on. I was about to put the kettle on as well,' said Joey, her voice barely a whisper.

Ruby noticed the broken sound. 'You all right, Joey?'

Joey kept her eyes on the bright yellow kettle. 'Just a bit tired this morning, Rubes.'

Ruby didn't look as though she were buying that.

Joey Walker was well known for being up before the birds. She grew up on the dairy farm that was on Pepper Lane, Pepper Pot Farm, so she knew all about the early shift.

Ruby put on her apron and washed her hands in the stainless-steel sink, enjoying the heat from the hot tap. She glanced around the kitchen, then peered out the doorway to the shopfront. 'It'll be busy out there tomorrow.' She sighed deeply to herself as she grabbed a green tea towel. 'Right, let's see how much we can get done today.'

Joey smiled at the sixty-six-year-old woman with the bright red hair. She loved working alongside Ruby, happy that she had given her the baking job six years ago when Wes had announced to his wife that he suddenly wanted a divorce.

Their son, Freddy, had been devastated, and Ruby was quite lost. Joey had to help her mum's old friend somehow.

Ruby was the only person in Joey's life who spoke fondly about her mum. Joey loved to hear the old school stories and what they got up to in their teens.

The only Walkers who lived up at Pepper Pot Farm with Joey were her big brother, Nate, his teenage daughter, Daisy, and their grandmother, Josephine. Her dad had died when she was nineteen, and her mum had left when she was a baby.

Joey secretly loved the woman who abandoned her, but she wasn't allowed to talk about her. The rest of her family hated her mum, as did most people in Pepper Bay. Everyone except Ruby.

Joey made them both tea, then started to weigh out some flour.

'Where's my list of things to do?' asked Ruby, peering over the top of her big round glasses. 'I know I left it here somewhere.'

Joey smiled and nodded over at the fridge. 'You put it there yesterday.'

Ruby chuckled to herself as she removed the pineapple fridge magnet that was holding her to-do list.

'Are we making up some small gift baskets today, or is that tomorrow?' she asked.

Joey didn't need a to-do list. She had everything logged in her mind. 'We can prep them today, but I want to add the biscuits in the morning.' She nodded to a cardboard box on the pine table in the middle of the room. 'Gran's given me some of her jam to put in.'

'Ooh, is that the one with the port in it? I'll take one of those home later.'

'That reminds me, Freddy wants some for the pub.'

Ruby nodded. 'I'll pop them over to him later. Not sure what time he's working over there today.'

'I've already made all the stuffing for Christmas, and Nate's put aside cheese and cream. Fred's already collected the eggs.'

'I love your stuffing, Jo. Best part of my Christmas dinner every year at The Ugly Duckling.' Ruby giggled. 'Don't tell

14

Freddy I said that. Bless my boy. He works so hard over there, and Christmas Day is so hectic with all of us lot there.'

'He loves it. He's the best chef. Anyway, that's why we all do our bit.'

'Yes, I've done the pudding, and the Sparrows will be supplying free booze all day, and we've got Jake Reynolds and his new lady helping out this year.'

Joey smiled warmly. 'Anna. She's so lovely. I'm glad Jake met her.'

Ruby's green eyes widened. 'Yes, and homeless, living on his rooftop in London, poor girl. And I heard what that ex of hers did too. Conned her out of the business she had with him. Bookshop, wasn't it? Terrible affair. Oh well, it all worked out for the best for her in the end. I'm glad she owns The Book Gallery now. She's a nice girl, and I don't want any of the shops in Pepper Lane to change.'

'Jake and Anna are in charge of the table decorations this year.' Joey giggled as she turned to face Ruby. 'If it's down to Jake, we'll probably be eating off gold plates.'

'Ooh, can you imagine.'

'I think Anna will do something magical. She's very creative. Did you know she's turning the flat above the bookshop into an art gallery?'

'That's a good idea.' Ruby started lining up her spoons and spatulas. 'More room for all those lovely paintings. Our Scott will be pleased. Some of those are his.'

Scott Harper. Not seen him in a while. If it weren't for Josh, I'd happily go out with him. Perhaps I'll ask him out next time he's here.

'I've not seen your nephew for the last couple of years, Rubes. What's he been up to?'

'He's been travelling with his work, but he's due back in a couple of months. Told me he's going to leave his job and

15

settle here. No doubt, he'll come over to check out The Book Gallery. He'll probably ask Anna for a job there, knowing him. He liked working part-time there once before, even with Betty Blake as his boss. Bless him. Patience of a saint.'

Joey laughed. 'I can't see Jake letting him work with Anna.'

Ruby waved a block of soft butter at her. 'Why not? What's wrong with my Scott?'

'Nothing, that's the point.' Joey started weighing some caster sugar. 'He's bloody gorgeous.'

'Aww, do you think so?'

Hell yeah!

'He's got that cute, geeky vibe going on. Clark Kent. I swear, every time he takes off his glasses, his chest rises and everything.'

Ruby giggled. 'Clark Kent.'

'Molly always went weak at the knees whenever he came in for his green tea. She'll be glad he's coming back.'

'Aww, our Molly. Nah, she's got designs on my Freddy. Anyone can see that. Except him, that is. What is it with some men? Blind as bats.'

Joey stifled a laugh. 'Designs.'

'When are you going to start meeting men, Joey?'

Joey snorted and poured too much sugar into the metal bowl on the scales. She started to spoon some back into the bag. 'Meeting men?'

'Pretty young girl like you should be out on the town.'

Joey felt her nose twitch. 'Young girl? I'm thirty-two now, Rubes. Anyway, when have I got time for all that? I work here all day and help out at the farm when Nate needs me.'

'You always seem to make time when Josh Reynolds is here.'

Joey stopped what she was doing and glanced over at Ruby, who carried on lining baking trays with baking paper and butter, pretending to act nonchalant about her statement. 'He's upstairs,' she whispered, flicking her eyes towards the ceiling.

Ruby's face fell flat. 'Oh, is he now?'

'Reckons he's here for Christmas. Said Jake asked him to come.' Joey frowned at herself. 'Why am I whispering?'

'You just remember how hurt you felt last time he left.' Ruby cut a strip of baking paper. 'You can't keep falling into his arms every time he's here.'

I don't plan to. Not this time. This time everything's going to be different. This time I'm going to be in complete and utter control of my feelings. I do not, in any way, shape, or form love Josh Reynolds any longer.

3

Josh

Edith's Tearoom smelled like fresh coffee and chocolate cake. Pink gingham tablecloths were the first things that caught Josh's eyes as he opened the internal door that led from the flat upstairs to the shop floor. He looked left and smiled warmly at the empty tea shop. His eyes bypassed the vintage bunting hanging in the windows either side of the shop door to peer outside at Pepper Lane. He saw light raindrops of greyish blues and hints of pale lavender. The colour of winter air. He immediately wanted to sit on the pavement alongside the narrow conduit that ran down the road towards the sea. He could feel his need to paint the picture he could see in his imagination.

Josh had enjoyed painting pictures, mostly of landscapes, and sometimes streets, all of his life. He would see one image, then create another vision inside his mind. His brushstrokes would reveal only what he could see.

His grandfather had wanted him to study business at university, but Josh flat-out refused, and his grandmother had stepped in and allowed him to follow his heart and gain a degree in art.

John Reynolds had hoped his grandsons would work alongside him, but neither one of them had shown much of an interest. He had never been in favour of the way his wife spoiled them, and he hated the playboy images they both portrayed to the world.

Standing in his grandmother's favourite place in the whole world filled Josh with love. His grandfather's coffee shop chain, Café Diths, had been his grandfather's dream, not his, nor his grandmother's, but she loved her husband and followed him to London to help him build the empire that Josh and Jake were both left with.

Josh was thankful that his brother had slipped into his grandfather's role, because the thought of working in an office drained his soul completely.

The Marshall family had lived in Pepper Bay for many years, and Edith Marshall had been the last to carry the family name. She was twenty-one when she opened her tearoom in Pepper Lane. She got to marry the man she loved, John Reynolds, have a son with him, who gave her two grandchildren, and she had come back to Pepper Bay at least once a year. She had lived out all of her dreams. Her dying wish was for her grandsons to live out theirs.

Josh took a moment at the shop door. His mind drifted to his parents. He struggled with memories of them. All of his most vibrant memories were in Pepper Bay with his brother and grandparents, and Joey Walker.

He pulled his eyes back into focus and slipped effortlessly into painting mode as he gazed through the glass.

A view from the tearoom.

His bright azure-blue eyes homed in on the pastel-yellow shop opposite.

Dolly's Haberdashery.

He stepped closer to the front door and stared through the light drizzle of rain to the old shop over the road that sold buttons and knitting needles, amongst other bits and bobs needed to make clothes and soft furnishings. He loved all the pastel, quaint shops in Pepper Lane.

He suddenly felt a presence behind him and the sensation of happiness.

Hello, Joey.

Joey looked over his shoulder. 'Poor old Doll. She won't last much longer. Told me her business has almost run dry. Sad, isn't it? Her niece is supposed to be taking over at some point. She might be able to turn things around for the shop. Apparently, her name is Dolly as well, so I'm guessing the shop sign will remain.'

He turned to face her and quickly pulled her into his arms, resting his head down onto hers. Her five-foot-seven height made it easier for him not to bend so much. At five-eleven, he wasn't that much taller than her.

I've missed you so much, Jo. God, I've missed holding you.

He started to stroke her back, but she pulled away.

'What are you doing, Josh?'

He nodded over at the window. 'Oh, I was just getting a painting idea.'

'Not that.' She took another step back. 'Holding me?'

What is she going on about?

'Erm… is there something wrong, Jo?'

He watched her hands wriggle together and one of her shoulders scrunch up awkwardly towards her neck.

'I don't want you holding me anymore.'

He just about heard her, her voice was that quiet. He glanced at his watch.

9 a.m.

'Five hours ago, I was in your arms, Jo.'

She lowered her eyes to the floor. 'I know, but you needed my help. You don't now, so I would appreciate it if you didn't touch me anymore.'

Josh was confused. 'As in anymore for a bit, or anymore forever?'

She swallowed hard and looked him straight in the eyes. 'Forever.' She sounded quite firm about it.

20

Josh felt his heart sink. 'But we always... touch.'

'I don't want to do that anymore, Josh. I made that decision the last time you left.'

What's changed? Something's changed.

'Have you met someone?' he asked.

Please say no. Oh God, Jo, please say no.

'No,' she replied.

He controlled the shaky breath trying to surface. 'Have I upset you?'

'No.'

'Can we talk about this?'

'No.'

He raised his brow. 'Really? You want to suddenly change everything about us, and you don't want to talk about it.'

He watched her awkwardness disappear in one second flat.

'I don't owe you anything.' Her tone was harsh and unforgiving. 'I haven't seen or heard from you in three years, and you just think you can swan in here and just... hold me.'

Josh opened his mouth to speak but realised he had no words. He slowly pursed his lips.

'And another thing,' she added quickly, 'put some bloody clothes on when you're staying in the flat.'

He glanced down at his jeans and jumper.

She rolled her eyes. 'I'm talking about you walking around in your boxer shorts last night. This morning. Whenever.'

Josh felt a bit gobsmacked. 'I was in bed. You were the one who walked in like a burglar. Sorry I didn't get dressed for the person I thought was robbing my gran's flat.'

Joey went to speak, but he raised his index finger in the air to silence her.

'You were the one who offered to hold me. I didn't ask you. I never ask you. You have always been the instigator in this…'

What do I call it?

'This what?' she asked through gritted teeth.

'Whatever this is,' was all he could manage.

'Well, now I'm un-instigating it.'

Josh didn't like the feeling of abandonment that had suddenly appeared in his heart. 'Is that even a word?'

'If it's not, it is now.'

'Well, perhaps you should have done all your un-instigating a long time ago. You know, like when we were sixteen and you kissed me for the first time. How about at seventeen when you took my virginity, huh, how about then?' He felt stupid as soon as the words left his mouth.

'Oh, I took your virginity, did I?'

Josh's eyes were wide with agitation. 'You know you did.'

Joey's angry face softened before him. He saw her drop her beautiful eyes and lower her head submissively.

'You wanted it too,' she whispered.

I wanted it then, and I want you right now.

He lowered his voice to match hers. 'I did.'

She stayed silent, and he was worried she was going to cry.

'I'm sorry I said it that way, Jo. I know you started it, but I sure as hell made sure I joined in. Even if I so much as hear the word *straw*, I think of us that night lying on the straw bales in your dad's barn.'

He watched the corners of her mouth curl. Her taupe eyes slowly rolled up and stopped at his mouth.

Oh God, Jo. If you really don't want me to touch you anymore, you'd better walk away right now, because I'm struggling here.

He cleared his throat. 'Erm, I was thinking I'd just pop up to Starlight Cottage to see Jake.'

He was pleased to see her eyes leave his lips. She was making her no-touching rule extremely difficult. He could stop himself from having sex with her, because that was part of his plan anyway, but not being able to touch her at all wasn't something he had visualised. It wasn't something that he wanted to agree to.

'I'll take you, if you want. Molly's just started work, so I'm due a break. My scooter is out the back.'

Josh grinned. 'You still got that old thing?'

'Well, if it's not good enough for you...'

'I'll take the ride, but you do know that it means I'll have to hold on to you, right?'

He watched her body still.

4

Joey

Josh's warm arms wrapped around Joey's waist as soon as he sat down behind her on her pale-blue scooter. She felt them tighten and one of his hands stroke over her stomach. His touch took away the dampness and the dullness of the cobbled alleyway at the back of Edith's Tearoom, surrounding her with sunshine.

I am so taking this man to bed in a minute. No you're not. Shut up. Concentrate. I can't do it. I can't do it. I love him. I want him. Argh! I'm going to punch myself in a minute. How is this so hard? Am I seriously that weak? What a joke.

'I'm glad you had your bike covered up, else we'd both have wet bums.' He leaned his head forward so that his cheek brushed across hers.

Oh, you have got to be kidding me!

A hundred butterflies left her stomach to fill her whole body.

I seriously can't do this. Yes, you can. Come on. Straighten up. You've got this. Push him off. Move, Reynolds.

She pushed back on him to move him, but her manoeuvre only encouraged him to push forward on her some more. She pulled her lips in tightly in annoyance and lifted her purple helmet and plopped it on her head.

Ha! How do you like that? You can't touch my face now. Oh, but he felt so good. His hot breath was down my neck. I actually want to cry right now. I can't cope. I'm just going to get off and take him to bed. No, you're not. Stop talking to yourself. Right, head up, face forward. Act natural. I just have to remember that he hasn't spoken to me in three years. Don't speak to him. Okay, it's too late for that. Just don't go all gooey. Be strong. Have some self-respect. I love me. I love me. No one is going to hurt me again. He does not belong in my heart. Yes. Right. Focus.

She felt him shift back a touch, and then he knocked on her helmet, making her frown. She ignored his laughter and started up the engine. She wobbled a bit trying to steer the bike out of the narrow alleyway, because having him sit behind her was making her nervous and causing her mind to go blank.

She could hear him laughing at her. 'Easy, Jo.'

She took a controlled breath and concentrated as she headed out to the road.

Pepper Lane was quiet. The winter kept most tourists away from the picturesque bay, with its chocolate box cottages and quaint little shops. The locals were all too busy with work and a fast-approaching Christmas.

Some of the homes had Christmas lights twinkling on them or along their driveways, switched on early to help bring some cheer to the gloom in the daytime sky.

Joey loved riding her scooter up and down Pepper Lane. She never had the confidence to ride her bike anywhere else, even though she loved the freedom she felt gliding through the air around her.

It was Josh who had got her into the joy of bikes back when they were in their early twenties. Although she was happy to cling on to him whilst sitting on the back of whichever fast motorbike he owned at the time, she would never go as fast on her own, not that her old bike could ever compete with the beefy engines Josh would buy.

The little blue scooter trudged along at 20mph, almost coughing its way uphill.

Joey was smiling widely under her helmet because she was in Josh's arms. She only wished it was the other way around.

Those were the days. He'd take me out on his bike. I'd hold on for dear life and love every moment being that close to him. We'd go all over the island, and I wouldn't want our day to end. Where did that time go? I can't believe we're in our thirties. I can't believe I have been holding on to him for this long. Why can't I just stop loving him?

She was going slower than normal because she wanted to be in his arms for as long as possible and because the road was wet, and she was worried about the fact that he wasn't wearing a helmet.

Josh started singing "My Boy Lollipop". His muffled voice was happily belting it out behind her.

She laughed to herself. One of her favourite things about Josh was how he would burst into song at any given moment and how those songs were always from the 1950s or 1960s.

She absorbed every moment of their journey as though it would be their last.

Starlight Cottage came into view as the bike huffed and puffed its way up towards the clifftop. The side extensions didn't take away the beauty of the original grey stone building that was the last cottage on Pepper Lane.

Joey pulled up outside the pale-blue, rustic gate that led to a stepping stone pathway that led to the front door.

He's going to leave me now. Nothing new there. Why do I do this to myself? What did I ever do to make him forget about me so easily? Why can't he love me? Why do I worry about this so much? Why does he make me feel so blue? I'm crazy. Great! Now I've got Patsy Cline in my head. Oh shut up, Jo, don't start singing.

Josh got off the back of the bike and immediately lifted off her helmet. He grinned at her messy hair, then slowly flattened it back down with one hand.

Joey felt her stomach flip.

Stop touching me, Josh. Please, stop touching me. You don't know how hard this is for me. I've started singing country songs, and I sure as hell am not going to stand by my man when he buggers off every five minutes.

She snatched the helmet from him.

'Bloody hell, Jo,' he said, laughing, 'could this thing go any slower? I could have walked here quicker.'

'We're not all adrenaline junkies, you know.'

He nodded behind him. 'If Jake hasn't got rid of my bike, it should still be in the garage. You want a ride?'

Love to.

'I have to get back to work,' she replied, trying to sound indifferent.

He's using his sexy side smile. I can't resist that look, and he knows it. I'm going to kiss him. No, I'm not. I'm stronger than this. I can do this. Sexy smile, be gone a while, run a mile from me. What the hell was that? Did I just cast a spell?

'I'll take you up to Sandly View,' he said, bringing her out of her thoughts.

He knows I love that place. I made love to him up there once. He's trying to break me, or wind me up. Well, he's not going to bloody well win.

'Another time,' she said, putting on her helmet. She watched him step closer and lean over the top of her head. 'Did you just kiss me?'

'Nope.' He knocked on her helmet. 'Wasn't you at all.'

Joey narrowed her eyes at him. 'Hmm! I'm off now. I'll see you later.'

'You will definitely see me later.'

She ignored the flirtatious look in his eyes.

I'm not looking. I'm not looking. My enchanted helmet is my forcefield. His charm cannot break through my trusty armour. I have seriously just turned into a witch. Gran will be pleased. I need to see her. She'll help me. She reckons she can see into the future. Well, it's time she looked into mine.

'Say hello to Jake and Anna for me.'

She watched the grin leave his mouth immediately as confusion washed over him.

'Anna? Who is Anna?'

Jake hasn't told him about Anna?

'Jake's girlfriend.'

Josh looked even more surprised. 'Jake has a girlfriend?'

Do you have a girlfriend? No, of course you don't. You wouldn't be here if you did. You might still have come here. Maybe you're on a break. Maybe you're hiding from her. Maybe you're bringing her here in a few days to introduce her to everyone. Maybe I need to shut up. I need to get away from him.

'I'll let him tell you about Anna. See you later.'

She rode away wondering why Jake hadn't told his brother about the woman he was in love with.

5

Josh

The small hallway was empty, and the renovated cottage was quiet. Josh peered into the oak country kitchen to his left, which was through an archway, and then he looked through the opened double doors that led to the living room to his right. He smiled warmly to himself as thoughts of his grandparents filled his heart.

Starlight Cottage was once a small three-bed cottage. John Reynolds had transformed the grey stone house a while back to get a good sale. He had added an extension on either side and one at the back, along with a detached double garage, and a swimming pool and cabin that were in the back garden. Edith had a change of heart once it was finished and couldn't bring herself to sell her old home, so it remained in their family. She would take her grandsons there every summer, and sometimes at Christmas too. Josh loved the old cottage, with all its mod cons and memories.

There was no sign of Jake or Anna.

They're probably out the back.

He made his way over the dark-wood polished flooring to the cloakroom. He opened the barn-like door, poked his head inside, and bent over to untie his boots.

Edith always made the boys change into their slippers as soon as they entered the cottage, so it was second nature for him to head straight for the cloakroom.

He felt someone tap him on his back. He straightened up and turned, and his eyes nearly fell out of his head.

There was a pretty woman with short dark hair and ice-blue eyes standing in front of him holding open the navy dressing gown she was wearing. 'Surprise!' she sang out, revealing her naked body.

Josh jumped and stumbled into the doorframe as she screamed and quickly wrapped herself back up.

'You're not Jake,' she just about managed to say.

Jake ran down the stairs, jumping the last three, to arrive swiftly at her side. He caught his breath as Josh caught his eye.

'Bloody hell, Anna,' he said, still panting. 'You scared the living daylights out of me.' He shot his brother a hard stare. 'Josh, what the hell are you doing?'

Me? I didn't do anything.

Josh went to speak, but Anna beat him to it.

'I thought he was you. He looks just like you,' she told Jake. 'I flashed him.'

Josh watched Jake's mouth gape open. He pulled in his lips to stop himself from laughing, as he knew that Jake would not take kindly to him thinking this was funny.

Jake looked like a cartoon character that had steam coming out of its ears. He glared at Josh. 'You saw her naked?'

Yep! Saw everything.

Josh shook his head slightly. 'No. I didn't see anything. It was all over within a split second. I was too shocked to notice.' He turned his eyes towards the embarrassed woman. 'Sorry.' He held out his hand. 'I take it you're Anna?'

Anna went to shake hands, but Jake slapped Josh's hand away.

'This isn't the way I wanted you two to meet.'

It was quite clear to both Josh and Anna that Jake's anger hadn't simmered yet.

'Josh, what are you doing here?'

'You invited me for Christmas. The Ugly Duckling. All the trimmings. Remember?'

Jake turned to Anna and wrapped a protective arm around her shoulder. 'Are you all right, Anna?' His voice was calm and caring, which made Josh raise an eyebrow. He wasn't used to seeing his serious brother look so affectionate.

Anna still looked quite dazed, but then she giggled. 'I'm okay, Jake. Guess it's a bit funny, when you think about it.'

Josh agreed and started to smile.

Jake wasn't smiling at all. He turned to Josh. 'It's not funny.'

Josh twisted his lips in a bid to control his grin. He turned his attention to Anna. 'So, Anna, make me a cup of tea and tell me all about yourself.' He led her towards the kitchen.

Jake quickly followed them. 'Make your own bloody tea.'

Josh sat down opposite them at the six-seater solid oak kitchen table. He really wanted to take the opportunity to tease his big brother, but he knew how serious Jake could be, and he wasn't sure just how far he could push him when it came to Anna. It was quite clear that Jake was deeply in love with her.

Jake and Anna locked arms on the table as they both leant forward slightly towards Josh.

Josh sat back, feeling as though he was the one who was about to be interrogated.

Hmm. This is new. How to approach this. Will Jake want me asking her questions? She seems nice enough, but I don't know her. How well does he know her?

'You'll have to excuse me, Anna, but Jake hasn't mentioned you, so why don't you tell me about yourself.'

Jake intervened, 'This isn't a job interview, Josh.'

Anna didn't seem to mind. 'He just wants to know who I am, that's all.'

Josh raised his hands towards her. 'See. We're just going to get to know each other.'

'Josh, Anna. Anna, Josh,' said Jake. 'There you go. That's all you need to know.'

He seems guarded.

Anna giggled. She gently stroked Jake's arm.

Josh watched a softness appear in his brother's eyes. It intrigued him to see Jake in such a different light. He knew his brother had never been in love before or brought a woman to Starlight Cottage, so obviously Anna was someone pretty special.

Anna reached her hand across the table. 'I'm Anna Cooper, I'm thirty years old, and I come from London.'

Josh smiled warmly at her and shook her hand. 'How do you do, Anna.'

Jake huffed. 'You sound like you're on a game show.'

Anna continued to smile over at Josh. 'I met your brother at his apartment in London. River Heights. I was living in a tent on the roof there. I fell in love with him pretty much straight away, and I owe him my life.'

Josh was still in shock over the rooftop story as he watched his brother rest his head on the side of hers.

'You don't owe me anything, Anna,' Jake whispered to her.

Josh was picking up on the intensity between them, but he was still slightly dazed, and it was distracting him. 'I'm sorry, the roof?'

Jake filled in the gaps about how Anna's ex had kicked her out of his home and bookshop business, leaving her homeless.

Josh was wary. He knew how women flocked to Jake for his money, because they did the same thing to him.

'So, now you live here with my brother?' He hoped his distrust wasn't showing in front of Jake. He had a strong feeling it wouldn't go down too well.

'Yes, we have moved here,' said Jake, looking Josh directly in the eyes.

'Jake bought us The Book Gallery,' said Anna, beaming up at Jake.

Did he now?

Jake didn't remove the hold he had with Josh's eyes.

Josh glanced at Anna. 'So now you have a home and a business, thanks to my brother.'

He watched Anna recoil.

'Yes.' She swallowed hard. 'He has been very kind to me.'

Josh could instantly tell that his brother did not like the slightly broken tone to her voice.

'It's not kindness, Anna,' said Jake softly, close to her face. 'It's love. I love you.' He then turned to Josh, and his softness disappeared. 'Anna and I have plans for our future. This is home now, and the people in this room are my family.'

Josh went to speak, but Anna's golden retriever came trotting in.

Jake nodded down at the dog. 'Including this one.'

'His name is Max,' said Anna, still looking awkward.

Max went straight over to Josh and nuzzled his nose into his lap.

Josh smiled warmly at the lovable dog making friends with him. 'Hello, boy.'

'He is very friendly,' said Anna.

'Yes, he is,' said Josh, roughing up his fur.

Anna obviously felt the need to say something to Josh. 'I love your brother, you know. Very much. I don't want his money.'

'Anna,' snapped Jake.

She turned to him. 'I guess people will think that, Jake.'

He cupped her face in his hands. Her dark bob flopped over the top of his fingers. 'Then they don't know you, and I don't care what they think. They don't matter anyway. All that matters is us.'

Josh watched Jake kiss her nose.

He's got it bad.

Max gained his attention again.

Josh slowly stroked the dog's head as he glanced over at the loved-up couple who looked one step away from the bedroom.

'I'm sorry I made you feel that way, Anna, but he's my brother. He might be thirty-five, but it's still my duty to worry about him. As I'm sure you already know, we own the coffee shop chain Café Diths, and it's a very lucrative business. Our money attracts a lot of female attention...'

Anna's giggle cut him off. 'Sorry. But I think you get a lot of female attention because of the way you both look. Have you looked in the mirror lately? You're bloody gorgeous.'

Jake cleared his throat as Josh grinned.

'Obviously, you're not as bloody gorgeous as my Jake. But then, nobody is in my eyes.'

Josh wanted to burst out laughing after seeing his brother blush. He quickly bit in his lip.

'Although,' she added, 'you do have a much friendlier face, Josh.'

Josh couldn't hold it in any longer. He burst out laughing as Jake frowned with amusement at her.

Anna was staring at Jake with nothing but love in her ice-blue eyes. 'But I love your serious face, Jake.'

Jake kissed her, making Josh feel as though he were suddenly invisible.

'Okay, you can stop that now.' Josh waved at them across the table. He waited for them to turn back to him. 'Anna, I can clearly see that you love each other very much. You have my blessing.'

Jake raised his brow.

Anna giggled. 'Thank you.'

'Welcome to the family,' said Josh.

Jake looked over at him. 'I would just like to point out that Anna was rebuilding her life on her own before I came along. She is an extremely capable person. All I did was show her Pepper Bay and…'

Anna interrupted, 'Change my life.' She gazed dreamily at him and whispered, 'I love you.'

Josh warmed inside at the love he could feel between them.

I'm not saying anything. Love is a mystery to us all. I guess you find it where you find it. There are no rules, not really.

'Are you going to stay here with us for Christmas?' she asked, turning his way.

'I can stay at Gran's flat. I don't want to be a gooseberry.'

'You won't be,' said Anna, taking charge of the situation. 'I want you to stay. This is your home too. We can all spend Christmas morning together. I've never had a family before, so I'd like that very much. I was raised in care, you see. I never had a forever home until I met your brother. He's my forever home. He's my forever everything. I know I might sound soppy, but I don't care. I'm never hiding my love for him ever again. It took me a while to tell him, you know. Anyway, will you stay?'

Josh smiled at her.

She's actually quite sweet.

'I'd like that.'

She turned to a smiling Jake. 'Well, that's settled then. This is going to be the best Christmas ever.'

Jake's azure-blue eyes were sparkling at her.

I can't get over the way he looks at her. I've never seen him like this. Ever.

'Shame Stan won't be here too,' said Anna. She turned to Josh. 'He's helping out at Crisis this year. Already had his name down and didn't want to cancel.'

'Who is Stan?'

'Anna's friend,' said Jake, before she had a chance to reply. 'He's more like a father to her. He works as the building manager at River Heights. I'm having a small cottage built for him on our land here. Hopefully, he should be here sometime in the spring.'

Wow, they really have got plans together.

Anna had a gleam in her eyes as she leaned towards Josh. 'Now, why don't you tell me all about you and Joey. Jake tells me she is the love of your life.'

Josh glared at his brother with amusement. 'Oh, did he?'

6

Joey

Joey hopped off her scooter and headed straight into the old farmhouse at Pepper Pot Farm.

The large chalky white building had been in her family for generations, and now her big brother, Nate, was the current owner. No one in the family had enough money to do all the much-needed repairs to the property. Its rundown appearance was something they had lived with for so long, they hardly noticed anymore. It had draughts and leaks, loose and stiff doors, old-fashioned furniture, and a temperamental boiler. The living room was the cosiest room in the home, with its large, grey-stone open fireplace, vintage lamps, and a long, extremely soft, brown sofa.

'Gran, you here?' she called out.

An old lady with broad shoulders and wispy strands of faded blonde hair walked past the kitchen doorway.

'In here, Joey,' she called back.

Joey entered the in-need-of-an-update kitchen and slumped herself down at the large pine table.

Her grandmother frowned over at her whilst closing a blue paint-washed cupboard door. 'What's wrong with you?'

Joey groaned. 'He's back, Gran.'

'Who is?'

'Josh.'

'Oh.'

Joey looked up. 'Gran, will you read my tea leaves? I need some help.'

'You know I don't dabble when it comes to my own family. There are some things the old Josephine Walker magic is not designed for. I can tell you one thing though. We're in for a hell of a time with that rain.'

Joey banged her head down on the table and groaned. 'Oh, Gran. Not a weather prediction again. How about something useful for a change, like a prediction for me.'

'No, Joey. I'm not looking into your future. No tea leaves. No Tarot. No nothing. There might be something I don't want to see.'

'Can't you just tell me the good bits?' she asked, her lips mumbling onto the wood.

'It doesn't work that way,' said Josephine, sitting down at the table. 'But you know what does work... talking.'

Joey slowly raised her head. There was little amusement in her eyes as she sighed deeply at her grandmother.

Josephine shrugged. 'Tell him you love him. It's not that hard. I told your grandfather that I loved him way before he ever said it back.'

'That's different. You both loved each other. Josh Reynolds doesn't love me.'

A faint crease added to the wrinkles on Josephine's brow. 'And whose fault is that, I wonder?'

Joey felt the dull ache of disappointment fill her body. 'Mine,' she huffed out.

Josephine nodded. 'You haven't given that boy any reason to think you love him. You throw yourself at him every time he's here, and then when he's leaving, you wave him goodbye as though you shared nothing together during his stay. If that were me, I would also think you were only interested in a holiday fling.'

Joey sat up straight. 'I only do that because I know he doesn't take us seriously. I'm not going to tell him the truth.

He'd never come back. He's not the serious relationship type.'

Josephine grumbled something under her breath and then said, 'How would you know?'

Fair point. I only know what he's like with me, but I've heard the rumours about him. Playboy Josh. Millionaire party boy. Spoiled heir to Café Diths. Models on his arm and in his bed. Clueless rich kid. Entitled, selfish, immature, that's what the papers said. Funny thing, I don't know that man. Josh is sweet and kind. He's funny and caring. We don't party. Never have. We just hang out. Have sex. A lot of sex. All I give him is sex.

'If he loved me, I'm pretty sure he would have told me by now.'

'That makes no sense coming from you, Jo.'

Joey reached her hands across the table and grabbed her grandmother's soft frail fingertips. 'Gran, I can't cope with this anymore. I don't know what to do. I'm losing my mind. I'm casting spells and living in Nashville.'

Josephine gave a rare sympathetic smile. 'Joey, dear, there are only two choices for you. You either tell him how you feel or you stick to your plan of getting on with your life without him in it ever again. That includes when he's here in Pepper Bay.'

Joey took a steady breath. 'It was a lot easier when he wasn't here for three years.'

'Who wasn't here for three years?' asked her brother.

Nate Walker stamped his dark muddy wellies on the concrete slab outside the backdoor of the kitchen. His large, muscular frame filled the doorway as he removed his wet black overalls.

'Who are we talking about?' he asked.

'Josh Reynolds,' said Joey.

Nate's cheery, chiselled face dropped into a disgruntled scowl. 'Oh no, not him again. I thought he was gone for good this time.'

Joey sniffed as the cold air from the back door hit her nostrils. 'Jake invited him here for Christmas.'

Nate stepped inside, swapped his wellies for black slippers, inscribed with the words *Best Dad*, and joined them at the table.

Josephine leant on his shoulder as she got up. 'I'll make you a nice cup of tea, boy.'

Nate put his arm around the back of Joey's chair. 'Do you want me to beat him up?'

She giggled, knowing he didn't mean it.

Nate smirked. 'I can set one of the cows on him.'

'Stop it, Nate.' She waved her hand at him. 'It's not his fault I end up heartbroken every time he leaves.'

'Fair enough.'

'I have told him that I don't want any sort of relationship with him this time.'

Nate widened his taupe eyes. 'Are you going to stick to it though?'

She stiffened her shoulders. A wash of determination flooded over her. She pursed her lips and gave a short sharp nod at her brother. 'Yes, I am. I have other plans for my life now.'

'Yes,' said Nate, 'like buying Honeybee Cottage. Any more news on that?'

She shook her head. 'No. Wendall said he'll let me know as soon as Loretta gives him the thumbs-up to sell. She was going to move before Christmas, but she's delayed it now till the new year. It doesn't matter. I'll still be the first to know, and I have my deposit ready and waiting and my mortgage approval.'

'I haven't got much, Jo,' said Nate, 'but I'll give any savings I have to help you start up. You know that, right?'

'Me too,' said Josephine. 'We'll have that place up and running for you in no time. We just need Loretta to hurry up and get lost.'

Joey gasped. 'Gran!'

Nate laughed. 'Poor old Loretta.'

Josephine placed a mug of steaming tea down on the table in front of Nate. 'Well, she needs to stop dithering and get a wriggle on. Our Joey's had her heart set on that place for years.'

'We can't force her out,' said Nate, blowing his tea.

'I reckon I can,' mumbled Josephine, leaving the kitchen.

Nate rolled his eyes over to Joey's glum face. 'Hey, it'll all work out how it's supposed to in the end.'

She smiled warmly. 'That's what Dad used to say.'

He winked. 'Dad was smart, that's why.'

Joey wished her dad was still alive. He would have made everything feel right again. He always knew what to say, and he had the best cuddles.

I wonder what my mum is doing right now. I wonder if she's thinking about me. Can she feel my pain? Does she just know whenever I'm feeling down? I wonder where she is. If she'll ever come home.

'You sleeping at Edith's tonight?' called out Josephine.

Joey looked over at the hallway. 'Yeah, I've got loads to do first thing.'

Nate groaned. 'Oh, I can't believe it's Christmas Eve tomorrow. Daisy's been giving me a headache going on about what she wants for Christmas all the time. Although, in some ways, that was helpful, because I didn't have a clue what to buy a thirteen-year-old girl. I've been having late-night Christmas discussions with Tess all month.'

41

'I wish you and Tessie would just get together. She shouldn't be living in The Ugly Duckling with her parents. She should be up here with you. Robyn sleeps here most of the time anyway, so what difference will it make if her mum moves in too.'

He widened his eyes, with a slight look of agitation set deeply within them. 'We're fine as we are, thanks.'

'But the four of you are like this readymade family, and Daisy and Robyn are more like sisters than cousins.'

'We're happy as we are.'

'Tessie hasn't been with anyone since Henry died, and that was, what, how old is Robyn now, thirteen, so yeah, thirteen years. You've been like Tessie's partner for the last five years. Is this because Henry's sister was Tessie's best friend?'

Nate scowled at the mention of Daisy's mum. 'Tori left when Daisy was a baby. Do you really think I would let her old friendship with anyone dictate my life?'

'I know, but you and Henry, and Tori and Tessie were so close growing up. I know you and Tess have only ever been friends, but you got closer than that when the girls were around three, and then you had to go and start dating and ruin any chances you could have had with Tess.'

'That was a long time ago.'

Joey nodded. 'That's what I'm saying. After the trouble Dana Blake caused this family over five years ago, you and Tess have been tight. I don't want you to ruin it again.'

Nate rolled his eyes. 'Don't let Gran hear you mention Dana's name in this house. The woman tried to marry me just so she could sell our home from under us, Jo. Gran has banned any mention of her. She almost lost one of her best friends because of that too.'

42

'Gran and Betty Blake always got on like a house on fire. I'm glad you-know-who didn't ruin that.'

'It can't be nice when you have a horrible kid.'

'Poor Betty, she's been put in a retirement village now. I know Gran misses her. Did you know her daughter put up the sale price on The Book Gallery when she found out Jake Reynolds wanted to buy the place?'

Nate sighed. 'Yeah, Jake told me.'

'I think you broke Tessie's heart when you went with Da... you know who.'

'I didn't. We've only ever been mates.'

Joey sighed deeply. 'Just kiss her, Nate.'

'Shut up. Daisy's upstairs, and I don't want her hearing stuff like that. She looks at Tess as a mother figure. I don't need her getting excited over something that is never going to happen.'

'Speaking of my beautiful niece,' said Joey, looking outside the kitchen. 'Make sure she's at the shop after lunch tomorrow for the gingerbread decorating.'

'Yep, we'll be there.'

'I'm coming,' said Daisy, entering the kitchen. She grabbed her long blonde hair and quickly scrunched its thick layers up into a knot on top of her head. Her big deep blue eyes twinkled towards Joey. 'I've got five friends coming over from Sandly. They all promised, and Robyn said she'll be there too.'

Joey stood up. 'Thanks, Daisy. Look forward to having you all. And that is exactly why I'm off now. I have so much gingerbread to make. Houses and families galore. I'll see you all tomorrow.' She bent over and kissed Nate on the cheek.

Daisy waved away an incoming kiss from her aunt.

Joey laughed to herself as she headed for the door.

'Mind riding in that rain, Joey, and keep away from Edith's grandson,' called out Josephine from the living room.

I'll try, Gran. I'm really going to try.

7

Josh

The puffy, floral, cream armchair in Edith's flat was Josh's favourite chair in the whole world. It was his grandmother's seat, and somewhere he would snuggle down into to read his comics when he was a boy. Just sitting there in that old seat filled him with warmth and love. He looked over his shoulder at the heavy rain on the other side of the sash window, grateful to be indoors. Tilting himself slightly to his left, leaning on the arm of the chair, he started to read his book.

Joey walked in and stood still when she saw him peacefully sitting there in his green-and-grey pyjamas.

Josh peered over the top of his tortoiseshell glasses. 'Hello, I thought everyone had gone home for the night.'

She seemed to hesitate before speaking. 'I'm... I was going to sleep here tonight. I have a lot to do first thing, what with it being Christmas Eve. I... I thought you would have moved into Starlight Cottage for the holiday.'

Josh lowered his book to his lap. 'I'm going there tomorrow. I wanted to spend another night here with Gran.'

'Oh.'

He watched her eyes sadly drop to the carpet. She turned to leave.

'Wait, Jo. You can still stay here.'

He waited for her to respond, but she didn't. She was still looking at the floor.

'I want you to,' he added softly. 'You can sleep in the spare room like you always do when you stay here, and I'll sleep in Gran's room.'

He saw her take a slow, deep breath.

'It'll be all right, Jo. We can share a flat for the night. We've shared a bed plenty of times. I'm sure we can do this, and even though you're the one who always pounces on me, I promise I won't pounce on you.'

She looked up and smiled.

That's better.

'I don't pounce,' she said, closing the door.

He grinned at her as she plopped her bag down on the table and made her way into the spare room.

'There's actually something I want to talk to you about,' he called out.

'Let me just get my pyjamas on,' she called back.

Josh glanced down at his book. He placed it down on the small pine table beside him and removed his glasses and put them on top of the back cover, then he pulled his dark-green dressing gown over his lap.

If I tell her about my new lifestyle, it'll make her feel more comfortable around me. She's definitely changed towards me. It's my own fault for staying away for so long. I reckon this will help. I don't like this awkwardness between us. It doesn't feel right.

'What do you want to talk to me about?' she asked, coming back in.

He swallowed hard as he watched her walk across the living room wearing red-and-white striped pyjamas. 'You look like toothpaste.'

Joey frowned and wrapped her arms around her chest as she sat down on the small beige sofa that was close to his chair. 'You're just full of compliments. It happens to be Christmassy, like a candy cane.'

Toothpaste? Seriously? What the hell, Josh.

'Best looking toothpaste I've ever seen, or candy cane.' He was hoping to lighten the mood.

Joey clearly didn't want to talk about toothpaste or candy canes. 'What are you reading?'

He glanced at his book. 'It's called A New Earth, by Eckhart Tolle.'

She looked genuinely interested, and that was one of the things he liked about her. She always listened when he spoke, and he could tell her interest wasn't fake in any way. He could speak openly to her about anything. She never seemed to look bored.

'What's it about?' she asked.

Okay, new life stepping forward in three, two, one...

'It's a self-help type of book. Spiritual. Teaches you about the ego, and the importance of being present. That sort of thing.'

Curiosity burned in her taupe eyes. 'I didn't know you read stuff like that.'

'That's what I want to talk to you about.'

'What do you mean?'

'Things have changed for me, Jo.'

'Like what?'

He shifted in his chair so that he was facing her. 'As I grew up, I turned into someone I was never really happy with. All that mattered was having a good time. Only, it wasn't a good time. Not really. All I did was party like there was no tomorrow. Nothing made sense. Then, when Gran died, I kind of went off the rails. I pretty much spent a year with my head stuck in a bottle. I was sleeping with different women, I couldn't even tell you their names, and, well, basically, life back then was one big meaningless blur. I had some sort of meltdown. It wasn't good.'

Silence loomed for a few seconds.

Josh thought she might have something to say, but she remained silent as though waiting for him to finish his story.

'Then I met someone,' he added. He saw her engaged expression disappear as her eyes suddenly glossed over.

'Go on,' she said quietly.

'A man called Rusty.' He was relieved to see a hint of a sparkle hit her eyes. 'That's his nickname. Anyway, he's like this spiritual guru type. He started to teach me some stuff, and then he spent more time with me, helping me to heal. Apparently, I needed a lot of healing.'

Joey smiled a smile that looked to be just for her.

'He took me to these retreat type places,' he added. 'I spent about a year and half at these centres. I learnt how to meditate. How to do yoga. How to breathe properly, because we're all doing it wrong, you know.' He breathed out a laugh.

'Has it helped you?' Her voice was low and gentle.

'It did. I stopped drinking. Stopped looking for quick-fix sex, that's what Rusty calls it. I went to these cleansing clinics. One checked me for sexually transmitted diseases. Not going to lie, Jo, that was both scary and embarrassing, but I got the all clear. Another clinic cleansed me with a really horrible liquid diet that I had to endure for a month. There was another that was to do with steam. It was to do with the outer layers of your skin. It's a bit more complicated than that, but you get the gist, and there was another one where I had to do a lot of talking.'

'Sounds like you've been through the mill.'

And then some.

He nodded. 'It really changed me. Made me feel as though I had uncovered the real me. The authentic me. I'd never felt so good my whole life. It was a real eye opener. I felt free. Trouble is, Jo, when Gramps died, I went and hit the bottle again.' He lowered his head and took a deep breath. 'I never slept with anyone. None of those women in my past ever meant anything to me anyway, so I didn't go down that road again. I'm never going down that road again. I was just drunk back then, uncaring about... about everything, really. I was so lost, I couldn't see where home was anymore, or who really mattered in my life. I really thought I had myself sorted, you know. I was so disgusted in myself for slipping back into the bottle like that. Everything I had learned went straight out the window.'

Joey leaned forward and placed her hand on his. 'Death is hard, Josh. You can't help struggling with that.'

'Jake asked me to come back here after Gramps died, but I couldn't,' he said, looking up at her. 'I was a mess. I ran as fast as I could back to Rusty. He was in New York. I stayed with him, and he helped me get back on track. I'm no expert on this healing malarkey, Jo, but I'm trying to sort my head out. I've felt like a different person since I met Rusty. I call him my mentor. He's great. So calming. He helps so many people.'

Joey smiled warmly and gave his hand a little squeeze. 'I'm glad he helped you.'

'So, I'm back off the booze, and I haven't slept with anyone since I met Rusty. That's what I wanted to tell you, Jo. I know you said you've got new rules for us, so I wanted you to know about my celibacy so that you would feel more relaxed around me. I sensed some awkwardness, and that's not like us at all. I just want you to know that you're safe with me. I'm happy for us to hold each other, but I don't want

49

there to be any sex for us, not that I put you in the same category as those women in my past. You're nothing like them. You know that what we have is different. I just thought that if I told you about my new lifestyle, you would feel better, but I understand that your rules are no touching at all, so I'll respect that.'

Her hand slipped off his as she sat back. 'Okay. That's good to know.'

He tried to read her expression, but she wasn't giving much away. She looked composed and nonchalant.

'So,' she added, 'how is the no sex thing going for you?'

Well, it was a lot easier when you weren't around.

He shrugged. 'Ah, you know. It's just sex, and that's not something I want in my life anymore.'

'What do you want for your life now?'

I want love, Jo. I want to make love to you like I have always done, but you don't know that. You think I was just having sex with you. Hopefully, one day, you might actually fall in love with me. I'm going to try and make you fall in love with me. I'm no longer going to be your holiday fling. I've come home. I'm staying, and I want to see if I can make things work with you, because you're the only girl I've ever loved. I'm back here for you. I'm ready to give you my all. I'm good enough for you now.

'I guess I want calm, stability, meaning. That sort of thing.'

50

8

Joey

*He doesn't want sex anymore. I guess that's it for us now.
Not sure how I feel. I don't think I like this. At least he's not
sleeping with anyone else. I didn't even know he was so
messed up. He's always seemed all right here, but that's all
I know about him, isn't it. I only know Pepper Bay Josh.
We've never been just friends before. I wonder if I can do
that. It shouldn't be too hard. We are friends. If I'm not
making love to him, will that stop me loving him altogether?
Look at him. He's beautiful, in every way. I love you, Josh
Reynolds. I don't think I'll ever stop.*

'Are you okay, Joey?'

She jolted out of her thoughts. 'Hmm? Oh, yes. I'm fine.
I guess I wasn't expecting to hear that.'

Josh gave a breathy laugh. 'What, the sex part or all of
it?'

She smiled warmly at him. 'All of it, I guess. So, are you
like some sort of spiritual monk now?'

The corners of his mouth curled. 'No. I just believe that
your body is sacred. We are made of energy, and we
shouldn't just combine ours with anyone else's just for the
sake of an orgasm. The other person's energy should matter
to you. You have to be careful who you allow into your
space, Jo. Some people are energy vampires. They're just in
it to drain you. I'm no longer in the business of sharing
myself. I have learned the importance of connection. Love is
what we should strive for.'

There was a slight moment where neither of them looked away from the other's eyes.

We're staring at each other for an absurd amount of time. This is getting silly now. We've just spoken about not touching, and now it feels as though we're going to completely ignore that conversation.

Joey had a sudden thought. She broke eye contact. 'I promise I won't pounce on you, Josh.' Seriousness flashed across her face. 'I wouldn't do that to you. I would never put you in a position that would disturb your healing in some way. I didn't want to have sex with you anymore anyway, so it's all worked out for the best, hasn't it?'

Oh shut up, Jo.

Josh sat back in his chair, staring forward at the kitchen. 'Yeah,' he said quietly.

Good grief, Jo, change the subject before you say something else that sounds dumb.

'Have you eaten yet, Josh? I brought some eggs up. I was just going to make an omelette.'

'I haven't had any dinner yet. I took some vegetables from Jake's earlier on. I was just going to make myself a quick stir-fry.'

'We could combine the two.'

He turned to her and smiled softly. 'I'm a vegan now, Jo, but you can put some of the veg in your omelette, if you want.'

She quickly grabbed her phone and sent Freddy a text. She wasn't sure if Freddy would have anything vegan on his Christmas dinner list.

Josh held an enquiring look. 'Who are you talking to?'

'Just Freddy Morland.'

'You two a thing now?'

Joey laughed, then quickly reeled in her smile as she could see that he was being serious. 'No. I was telling him you're a vegan. He'll make you something separate for Christmas dinner now.'

She watched him blush.

'Oh,' he said. 'Erm... he doesn't have to worry about that.'

'Are you kidding, he'll love making something else. Whatever he makes, I'm going to taste it too.'

'Hey! You keep your hands off my dinner.'

They both stared in silence over at the small kitchen. Neither of them moving.

'So,' said Joey, shifting her weight further into the sofa, 'are you like a Russell Brand type now?'

Josh grinned. 'Not quite. He has better hair.'

She quietly laughed, feeling so much better now that they were acting normal again, even if that didn't include them ending up in bed.

Josh got up. 'Come on, let's make that dinner now, then I can beat you at a game of Scrabble, like I always do.'

She stared at the hand he was offering her.

'I think we're both safe if you hold my hand, Jo.'

She took the hand that was wiggling at her, and her heart flipped as he closed his fingers around hers. She loved his hands. She remembered when they were teenagers and he was starting to change from a boy into a man. She would stroke his palm and tell him how much bigger his hand was to hers, and then they would both stare at the difference before staring at each other.

She remembered the first time he held her hand. It was the day after she had taken him by surprise by kissing him for the first time. She asked him if he wanted to go swimming at the beach in the morning. It was there that he grabbed her hand and ran into the sea with her.

Ruby owned one of the beach huts in Sandly back then. She had given Joey the keys for the morning. Inside that pink-and-green stripy hut was the second time Joey kissed Josh. Again, it took him by surprise, but that time he held on to her longer. He kissed her slower than the first time, and it was filled with so much meaning that she knew they were ready to take things further, but she waited. Sleeping with Josh was easy in her dreams, but the reality would be daunting. She wasn't sure what it would mean for them if they went that far. She just knew that she loved him so much, and she wanted to share everything with him.

She smiled to herself at the memory of awkwardly buying condoms for the first time.

Josh laughed, jolting her out of her thoughts.

She was pulling a plastic container filled with eggs out of her bag with one hand.

'You know we can't cook with one hand, right, Jo?'

She glanced down at his fingers still wrapped around hers.

I don't want to let go, Josh. I want to go back in time when things were… Actually, I'm not sure what was easier, then or now. Sometimes, it seemed as though you loved me back then. Oh, I don't know what to think anymore.

Hoping the heat she could feel in her face wasn't shining through her cheeks, she reluctantly let her hand slip from his. 'Sorry, I was away with the fairies.' She stared down at the eggs, not knowing how to feel.

He turned to the small white oven. 'Joey, I know I said I never ask you, and I know you have your rules now, but will you sleep in my bed with me tonight?' His voice was low and slightly unsteady.

She turned to face the back of him, wanting so badly to put her arms around him and hold him tightly.

God, Josh, you have no idea how much I want you right now. It's taking every ounce of willpower I've got not to reach out and...

'Yes, I can still help you sleep, Josh.'

A vulnerability sat in his eyes as he turned to her. 'I'll have to take my pyjamas off, but I'll put on a pair of boxers. Is that all right?'

She gently nodded. 'That's fine, but I'm sure you won't sweat tonight. You'll be okay with me there.'

He smiled, but it was weak. 'Thanks, Jo.' He took his dressing gown off and wrapped it around her.

She stepped forward into his hold on the nightwear. 'I'll always be here for you, Josh. You know that, right? We can have as many rules as there are laws, but that's the one thing that will never change.'

Josh's smile strengthened. He raised his hand to tuck a strand of her hair behind her ear. 'Hey, Jo?' His voice was soft and filled with warmth. 'We can still be friends, right? That is what you want, isn't it?'

She nodded and faked a smile. 'Yes, that's exactly what I want.' A twinge of guilt hit her straight in the chest for lying to him.

9

Josh

Josh woke to an empty bed. He knew he would. It was Christmas Eve, and Joey was expecting around twenty-five people from the Hotel Royale tour sometime that morning, and then a group of kids were due in after lunch for gingerbread decorating, which he had decided to join in with. He loved watching Joey work. Her cake decorating skills were every bit as good as her baking skills, and it always left him in awe of her. Sometimes, he would sit in the corner with his drawing pad and sketch her at work, pretending he was mindlessly doodling ideas.

He stretched out and smiled. He'd had the best sleep and felt refreshed and ready for his day. He glanced up at the ceiling. It was pretty quiet in the flat. He had been well and truly warned about how noisy it would get downstairs, but there wasn't any muffled sounds coming from below. He sighed deeply, not wanting to get up and face the day. He felt far too content.

All night he had slept with Joey by his side, and although they kept to their allocated sides and he'd struggled with not holding her, he was still happy that they had shared the night.

When she looked into my eyes last night, I swear she was going to kiss me. I know that's what I wanted. I had no idea I had that level of willpower in me. Even when she closed her eyes, I just wanted to reach across and hold her, stroke her face, tell her I'm hers. Oh God! I need to get up. Think of the positives. We're still friends. She still helps me sleep. I'm grateful to have shared last night with her. It's a good start.

I'm thankful that the universe brought us together in the first place.

He glanced down at his half-unpacked suitcase and quickly jumped out of bed to sit on the floor in front of it. He rummaged his hand through his clothes to find the two small Christmas gifts he had brought with him.

I'm going to have to buy Anna something as well now. What can I buy her? I haven't got much time.

He held on to the two gold-paper-wrapped boxes.

At least Jake and Joey are sorted. What do you get for someone you don't know? What do I know about her? She lived on a roof. She seems to like books. She always wanted a family. Ah ha! I've got it. I need to see Tessie. She'll have what I need, and then I'll pop into Dolly's. Right, let's get this day started.

He headed for the bathroom to get ready. Stepping into the bath, he switched the old shower on and smiled.

Not quite the power shower, but it works. I'm free. I'm at peace. I'm heading in the right direction. I know what I want. I'm taking my steps. Life is good.

He started to sing the Nina Simone song that popped into his head, "Feeling Good".

Joey came bursting in the bathroom. 'Josh.'

He poked his head around the white shower curtain. Water and shampoo was dripping from his face. 'What is it? What's wrong?'

She slumped down on the closed toilet seat. 'Pepper Bay is flooded. The river has come up too high. The tourists can't get through. Their minibus can't come down Pepper Lane, as there's a mound of water washing downhill. The tram, obviously, isn't running, and we need more sandbags for all the shops.' She took a deep breath. 'Oh, Josh, it's such a mess. There's an inch worth of water on the shop floor. It came in both doors, front and back. We got some more sandbags from the pub, but they need them too. We've not had a flood like this in years. Why did it have to happen today?'

Josh tried to blink away the shampoo from his stinging eyes. 'Don't cry, Jo. Give me one minute, and I'll help.'

She sniffed and blew her nose on a piece of toilet roll as he quickly went back to finish his shower.

Within five minutes, the shower was switched off, and the curtain was swiped back. Josh jumped out of the bath and quickly grabbed a large pink towel from off the top of the white plastic laundry basket.

He was well aware she was watching him quickly dry off.

The bathroom was quite small, so when Joey stood up, she was standing right in front of him.

He tried to ignore that fact and continued to quickly dry himself.

Jo, you're killing me. Step away. Please.

He wrapped the towel around his waist, squeezed past her, and headed for the bedroom to get dressed.

'What can I do to help?' he called out.

She stood in the doorway. 'I don't know. Grab a mop. Actually…' Her voice trailed off.

Josh was dressed in dark jeans and a black tee-shirt. He quickly tucked his top in as he entered the living room.

Joey was in a long cupboard in the kitchen. She pulled out a mop. 'Yay, we've got another one.'

He smiled as she turned to face him. He threw on a dark-brown jumper and gave her a slight nod.

She handed him the mop with one hand whilst answering her phone with the other. 'Okay, Anna. I'll send Josh over now with a spare mop.'

'Over where?' he asked.

Joey hung up. 'Nate got Anna down as far as the car park at the top of the lane using his tractor. She's decorating the pub today for our dinner tomorrow. She just said that the basement is deep in water, and they're trying desperately to pump it out. We're lucky we're on a slope, but it's still pouring through as far up as Roseberry Cottage to get to the sea at the bottom. I told her you'd go over. They've got it worse than us because of their basement. Jake will feel better if you're there too. He's been freaking out all morning, thinking Anna's going to drown or something. He's so protective of her, especially since what happened to her during the snowstorm we had a few weeks back.'

Josh was trying to keep up with everything he had missed. 'What happened to her during the snowstorm?'

Joey's eyes widened dramatically. 'It was terrible, Josh. She got trapped outside in it. We thought she had hypo-what's-it. We had to call the doctor and everything. Jake was a mess. Thought she was going to die. She wasn't that bad, but you know what Jake is like. She had fully defrosted by morning, but it still scared him.'

'Bloody hell. He didn't tell me. Mind you, he didn't even bother to tell me Anna existed. Have you seen the pair of them together? The way he looks at her, Jo. I've never seen him loved-up before.'

'Oh God, yes. He thinks the world of her. She's good for him, you know. He's a lot softer around the edges since being with Anna. And being back here, I guess. They're so happy. I'm glad they met. I knew he liked her from the first time I saw them together. He was trying to hide it, but it was so obvious. Well, it was to me.'

'Where is he now?'

'Nate's bringing him down, but they're stopping off at the cottages to see who needs help. Anything below the river line is pretty much flooded.'

'Your place is all right then.'

She nodded. 'So is Starlight. Luckily, we're up on higher ground above the river.'

'Come on. Let's get downstairs.'

Joey led the way.

Josh heard his boot squelch as it hit the shop floor. He looked around to see that no one else was down there. 'Where's Ruby and Molly?'

'Ruby's stuck in Roseberry Cottage, no doubt trying to save her floors and furniture, and I told Molly not to bother coming in. Fred offered to bring her round from Sandly in the boat, but there's no point in her coming out in this. I know it only takes five minutes to come around the bay, and Freddy knows what he's doing with his dad's boat, but she shouldn't risk it for nothing. We won't be having any customers today.'

A faint crease appeared between his eyebrows. 'Have you been down here all morning on your own dealing with this?'

She gave a slight nod. Her frazzled face looked ready to burst into tears.

He quickly grabbed her into his arms and held her tightly. 'Why didn't you wake me?'

Her mouth was pressing into his jumper. 'I don't like to wake you when you're sleeping well.'

Josh held her away from him and kissed her forehead. 'I don't care about sleep,' he said softly. 'If you need me, you wake me. Got it?'

She nodded and fell back into his hold.

He patted her back. 'Come on, let's sort this place out and then get over to The Ugly Duckling.'

Joey glanced over towards the back door. 'I've placed the sandbags. It's not so bad in here now. You go over the road and help. I'll stay here.'

'No, we'll both go. I'm not leaving you here on your own.'

'I'm okay.'

'You're upset, Jo. I want you with me. This place can wait. Like you just said, it's secure enough for now. Let's go help the Sparrows. They need us more.'

She gave a slight shrug. 'Okay. Run upstairs and grab your coat. It's pouring down out there. Put a hat on. You'll get a chill with your hair still damp. I've got my coat in the kitchen. Meet back here in thirty seconds.' She gave him a smile that warmed his heart.

Josh did a quick salute. 'Roger that, Captain.'

Joey giggled, then lost her smile again. 'Oh, Josh, Christmas will be ruined.'

He grabbed her hand as she turned to walk away. 'No, it won't, Jo. I promise.'

10

Joey

The Ugly Duckling was at the top end of the Pepper Lane shops. The old pub, with its white washed walls and dark-wood beams, had taken in a lot of river water through the cellar door that was built into the pavement around the side. The owners, Elaine and Ed Sparrow, had built a small wall of sandbags around the cellar door, forcing the rushing water to flow in a different direction. The basement was flooded, but at least there was less water pouring in since the emergency wall was put in place.

Elaine and Ed were pumping out water from below the pub floor with their daughter, Tessie, when Joey and Josh walked in.

'Oh no!' cried Joey.

Tessie's long, curly, red hair was scrunched loosely on top of her head. Tendrils were hanging around her flushed face. She quickly handed her best friend a bucket filled with water. 'Chuck this outside, Jo.'

Josh rushed forward and grabbed the black bucket and tossed the water out of the front door.

'There's plenty more where that came from,' said Tessie, looking back down the basement stairs.

Joey looked over at the back door to see Anna on her knees, struggling to adjust sandbags along the threshold. She turned to Josh. 'I'll help Anna, you help Tess.'

Josh nodded and went to peer down the stairs at the flood in the basement.

'Good to see you, Josh,' said Tessie, patting his arm.

Joey watched Josh give Tessie a quick kiss on the cheek before lowering his arm to take another bucket load of water from Ed, who was on the basement stairs.

'Good timing, Joshua,' called out Ed.

Joey went over to Anna. She dropped to her knees at her side.

'Your jeans will be as soaked as mine now,' said Anna, looking at her wet knees.

'Oh, what a mess, Anna.' Joey helped lift a sandbag, sliding it along on top of another.

Freddy came out from the kitchen. 'Nate's taken a load of sandbags up to the riverbank with some of the others. Hopefully, they can redirect the flow.'

Joey turned to Anna. 'I hope that works. We can't take much more.'

She nodded. 'It's a good thing we're on a slope, but that doesn't help much here, not with that basement.'

'We've been on at the council for years to build up the riverbank, but do they listen? No. Now look.'

Anna wrapped her arm around Joey's shoulders. 'We'll fix it, Jo. It's going to be all right.'

Joey smiled warmly at her. 'I admire your optimism.'

'How is it over at your shop?'

Joey shook her head. 'Just floor damage. Luckily, we don't have a basement. Insurance should cover that.'

'Don't worry if they don't. Jake won't let anything happen to his grandmother's shop. He'll make sure everything's put right again.'

'What about your bookshop, Anna?'

Anna lowered her arm and sighed with relief. 'We'd already had all the books and paintings moved upstairs because of the decorating we're doing in the new year.'

Joey was pleased. 'That's good.' She peered over her shoulder at Tessie and Josh. 'Poor Tessie, she looks ready to drop.'

'The Sparrows haven't stopped all morning.'

Joey and Anna stood up and went over to Tessie.

'What about if we make some sort of production line,' said Joey. 'It'll be easier on everyone if we pass the bucket to each other.'

'Good idea,' said Tessie, passing Josh another bucket.

Josh handed it to Joey, who handed it to Anna, who threw it out the door.

Anna glanced down at her feet. 'It's still coming in a bit, but the sandbags have done a good job at redirecting the flow. It's more in the middle of the street now. Good thing we've got the sea at the bottom.'

'Don't cry, Mum,' said Tessie, peering down the stairs.

Josh looked over her shoulder. 'Come up here, Elaine. I'll swap places with you.'

Elaine's short white hair appeared just above the cellar doorway. Josh reached his hand down as Tessie moved to the side to get out of her mum's way.

'Come on, Elaine,' said Josh softly, leading her up the rest of the stairs. He gave her one of his cheeky grins. 'Still rocking the Annie Lennox look, I see.'

Elaine smiled weakly and gave him a peck on the cheek as she passed him by.

Joey watched Josh disappear below as she quickly wrapped her arms around Elaine.

Elaine's blue trousers were soaked up to her thighs.

'Oh no, look at you,' said Joey, leading her over to a chair. 'Your legs are completely soaked.'

Elaine looked up at her. 'That's why I didn't send our Tess down there. It would have been up to her neck, size of her.'

Joey giggled at Elaine trying to lighten the mood.

'Oi! I heard that. It's not my fault I'm only five-foot-nothing,' called over Tessie.

Joey glanced over at Freddy. 'Fred, put the kettle on for Elaine, please.'

As soon as he entered the kitchen, the electricity went out.

'Electric's gone,' shouted out Ed.

Tessie looked down into the darkness of the basement. 'I'll get a torch, Dad.'

'I've got one in the shop,' said Joey. 'I'll just go get it. You're going to need more than one.'

'Good thing it's daytime,' said Elaine. 'We'll only need the light for the basement.'

Freddy walked out of the kitchen to stand behind the bar. He ran his hand through his hair, moving his apricot curls off his forehead. 'Depends how long this power cut lasts.'

Elaine put her wet hand on her head, squishing her fingers into her temple. 'Oh God, Christmas is ruined.'

Tessie's thirteen-year-old daughter, Robyn, came running down the stairs from their home above the pub. 'Mum, my computer went off.'

Tessie sighed. 'The electric has gone. You'll have to read a book or something.'

Robyn's pale-lavender eyes stilled. 'A book? That's your answer to my crisis.'

'In case you haven't noticed, Robs, we've got our own crisis going on here.'

Robyn went over to her gran and snuggled under her arm.

Elaine stroked the girl's long strawberry-blonde hair.

'You all right, Gran?' asked Robyn.

'Of course,' sang out Elaine, flapping one hand in the air. 'Go back upstairs and play a game on your phone or one of those fancy gadgets you've got that won't need charging in the next hour.'

Robyn rolled her eyes over to her mum. 'Can't I go up to the farm instead?'

Tessie shook her head. 'Not at the moment. Go upstairs and call Daisy, make sure she's all right. She'll be worried about her dad out in this weather trying to stop the flood. You know what she's like.'

Robyn removed herself from her gran and went back up to her bedroom to call Daisy.

Freddy's phone rang. 'It's Mum,' he told everyone. 'Hang on, Mum, let me tell them. She says the whole of Pepper Bay is out. No one's got any power.'

Elaine almost cried.

Joey leaned over and hugged her. 'It's going to be all right, Elaine. I promise. We'll fix everything. The water will stop soon, and if we have no electricity by tomorrow, then so what. We'll use Ruby's gas oven to cook a turkey, Fred can fry some chips on your gas rings out back, and I'll make a salad.'

'Sounds like a good plan,' said Freddy, putting his phone away in his back pocket.

'I still have all the table decorations,' said Anna. 'We'll put the fire on and dry out this floor, line the tables up, and have the best Christmas dinner ever.'

'It'll be great, Mum,' said Tessie.

Elaine smiled up at the girls. 'Well, we've got plenty of booze to drown our sorrows. Thanks, everyone.'

'We're not going to let this beat us,' said Joey, with sheer determination flashing in her eyes.

Elaine jumped up to her feet. 'Joey's right. A little bit of water damage isn't going to own us. Right, let's get back to it.'

Tessie chuckled at Joey. 'A little bit?'

Joey shushed her, then said, 'I'll just get that torch.'

Anna joined her side. 'I have one in my shop as well. I'll bring it over.'

Joey and Anna rushed outside to see that the rain was still pouring down, and the road looked like a water slide.

'Mind how you go, Anna,' said Joey, sprinting towards Edith's Tearoom.

Anna turned to head off to her own shop.

'Argh!' Joey cried. She had slipped in the rushing water and was sliding towards the shingle beach.

'Joey!' screamed Anna, running towards her.

Joey watched as Anna fell to her hip and skidded down to her side.

Anna grabbed Joey's arm and dragged her over to the pavement.

Joey gasped. She flopped her hand down to smack the water they were sitting in. 'Could we be any wetter?'

Anna laughed. 'This would make a great water slide on a nice summer's day.'

Joey burst out laughing as Anna flopped back to lie on the ground.

'I surrender,' she yelled out.

Joey joined her side, yelling up at the gloomy sky. 'You can flood our streets, but you'll never take our freedom.'

The two women roared with laughter as the rain poured down on them.

A tall figure holding an umbrella leaned over their bodies.

'What do you think you are doing?' snapped Jake.

'Oh, hello, Jake,' said Anna casually. 'Could you just fetch the torch from the shop, please. It's on the electricity box.'

Jake's stern expression did not soften one bit.

Joey sniffed. 'We fell over, but we're all right. We're getting up now.' She huffed and helped Anna to her feet.

Jake's bright eyes rolled with agitation over towards Joey. 'Could you take Anna up to Gran's flat and find her some dry clothes to wear. I know you have clothes there, Jo. You both need to dry off before you get ill. It's freezing out here.'

Joey flicked water at him from her wet fingertips. 'Yes, sir.'

Anna turned to him and fluttered her lashes. 'Don't be mad, Jake. We were just cracking up, that's all. Can't be helped sometimes.'

Joey watched Anna reach up to kiss him. She smiled to herself as Jake's serious face immediately changed to a look of sheer bliss.

Wow! He just melted. Just like that. I wish I could make Josh look at me that way. He has done, I think. Oh, maybe I'm just imagining things. That's all I need, to start rewriting history. I don't want to be that person. I want to remember exactly how everything was between us. He does look at me like that sometimes. I'm sure he does.

Anna turned and linked arms with Joey. 'The power's out, so Ed needs some light in the basement. I'll just get some dry clothes on and meet you back over there in a minute, Jake.'

Jake handed her the pair of wellies he had brought her.

'Where's my brother?' he asked.

Joey pointed over at the pub.

68

11

Josh

A bucket full of water splashed Jake's ankles as Josh tossed it out the door.

Jake's mouth gaped open as he looked down at his Chelsea boots.

Josh pulled in his lips in an attempt not to laugh, but it was no good. 'Sorry, Jake, didn't see you there.'

Jake sniffed and walked inside the pub. He stared up at the Christmas tree standing on a table over by the back door, then looked around at the rest of the tinsel-adorned place.

Freddy was lighting the fire, Elaine was standing on the basement stairs, and Tessie was taking the empty bucket back off Josh.

'Have you seen Joey?' Josh asked Jake. 'She only went to get a torch.'

'She's getting changed first. She fell over outside.'

Tessie gasped, and Josh's face paled as though he'd just seen a ghost.

'She's all right,' added Jake swiftly. 'She'll be back in a minute.'

Josh's worried eyes were on the door.

'Josh, she's fine. I promise you.' Jake looked over at the top of Elaine's tuff of white hair poking out of the basement. 'Now, where do you need me?'

'You can take over from Ed in a minute,' called out Elaine. 'He needs a break.'

'I'm all right,' shouted up Ed.

Elaine climbed up a step to look at Jake. 'He's not,' she mouthed.

'We're just waiting on some light,' said Josh, 'then you can come down there with me, Jake.'

'How's Nate getting on?' asked Tessie.

Jake looked pleased to give some good news. 'He and the others are making good progress. He sent me down here to check on you.'

Tessie smiled and walked away to warm herself by the fire.

'It's going to get very cold in here soon,' said Josh. 'We need that electricity back on.'

Jake pulled out his phone. 'I'll call the council.'

Elaine laughed. 'Good luck with that. It's Christmas Eve. There won't be anyone there.'

Josh pulled his brother to one side. He kept his voice low and his eyes on the door. 'We have to do something, Jake. No one's got electricity. It's going to get really cold soon. Everyone's got a fridge full of Christmas food that will go off, and now people are starting to get hurt.'

I need to see Joey.

Jake placed his hand on Josh's shoulder. 'Joey's all right, Josh. I wouldn't have left her if she was hurt. You know that. She was laughing outside in the street with Anna. Now, she wouldn't be doing that if she was hurt. As for everything else, what do you suggest?'

Josh could feel the bewilderment creeping up on him. 'I don't know. Old me would have jumped behind the bar and drank straight from the optics till spring arrives. New me is grappling with half-dead brain cells, desperately trying to compile some sort of helpful list. These people are like family to us. We have to do something.'

'We are doing something, Josh. We're helping them.'

'I feel bloody useless, Jake. We have all this money, surely we can do something with it to help. What do people normally do during a flood? What about if we fly them out to somewhere hot, or bring a yacht around to the bay, or take them for their Christmas dinner next door in Sandly? Hotel Royale, maybe? What about Frankie Law's restaurant over in Poole. We can get everyone there for Christmas.'

Jake moved his brother further out of everyone else's earshot. 'Josh, they are proud people. They won't want our money or anything fancy from us. All they need is for us to be here with them, helping them dry out this place. This is their home. Let's just wait and see how things are by tonight. The electricity might be back on by then.'

I feel bloody useless.

Josh didn't feel like waiting around. He wanted to make everything right for everyone straight away.

'Nate's just called,' said Freddy, waving his phone in the air. 'He said they've managed to block the part of the river that comes our way, so we should see signs of slowing water outside any minute.'

Everyone rushed to the door and windows to peer out at the wet street. The river water was no longer rushing towards the sea, and the rain had eased off a touch as well.

'Hey, it looks better already,' said Tessie.

Elaine huffed. 'Thank God for that.'

Josh looked over the road to see Joey and Anna standing in the shop doorway. He smiled as Joey waved over at him.

She looks fine. Beautiful as ever and absolutely fine.

'We just need to get the rest of the water out of the basement and dry this place out before we end up looking like one of those grotty dives,' said Elaine.

'Or smelling like one,' said Ed, popping his shiny bald head up from the basement. He grinned widely, revealing his one gold tooth in amongst his perfect white teeth.

Tessie came away from the window and wrapped her arms around herself. 'Let's all hope we don't freeze to death tonight.'

'We'll be all right,' said Elaine. 'We've got a fire upstairs as well, and you can take Robyn and sleep up at Nate's tonight. Me and your dad will be just fine here.'

'I'm staying at Mum's tonight,' said Freddy. 'You and Ed can sleep up at Roseberry with us, if you like. I'll cook us something nice in Mum's gas oven. We'll be all right.'

Josh spun around to Elaine. His eyes wide and hopeful. 'We have a portable generator in the shed up at Starlight. Not sure if it works. It's about three hundred years old, but if it does, we can bring it down here and attach some heaters and get this floor dried out as best we can ready for Christmas Day.'

Tessie beamed over at him. 'That might work. Well done, Josh. I know Nate has a generator, but that's for the farm. We won't be able to use that, but if your one works, it's worth a shot, and, Mum, I'm not going anywhere. We're spending Christmas morning together, like we always do.'

Elaine smiled at her daughter. 'Thanks for the offer, Fred, but we're all staying here.' She then looked straight at Josh. 'Won't you need that generator for yourselves?'

Josh shrugged away her worry. 'We'll be all right. We've got a fireplace up there too and plenty of logs. We'll be nice and warm, and Anna used to live on a roof, so she's used to the cold.'

Jake shot him a stern glare, which made Tessie muffle her giggle.

Joey was in the doorway. She had changed her clothes and was holding a torch. 'What's funny, Tess?'

'Oh, nothing. I'm just going to call Nate. See if he can get Starlight's portable generator working and bring it down here.'

Anna slid around Joey. 'Ooh, that's a good idea. There's an old electric heater in the shop. You can plug that in. We can take turns drying out Pepper Lane once the pub is sorted.'

Jake pulled her under his arm for a loving embrace.

Josh stared at them for a second.

I still can't get over the way he looks at her. They are so much in love. I wish that was Joey with me.

He rolled his eyes over to Joey, who was passing a torch to Tessie. He wanted to reach out and pull her into his arms. The thought process caused his body to gravitate a step closer towards her.

'I heard you took a tumble outside,' he whispered. 'Are you all right?'

He jolted slightly as she turned, as her face was so close to his.

'Bit of a bruised bum,' she said, trying not to giggle too loudly.

Josh's eyes creased at the corners as he looked down at her bottom. 'I can take a look at that later on, if you like.'

He watched her cheeks flush and found it highly amusing, because she hardly ever revealed any embarrassment.

Her bashful expression quickly disappeared as her confident eyes rolled slowly up to meet his.

Josh felt his stomach flip.

'We'll see,' she said quietly.

12

Joey

It was the night before Christmas, and every home in Pepper Bay had a log burning in their open fireplace. Candles lit every room, and those lucky enough to have a gas oven had been busy cooking meals for their neighbours. Families snuggled together in their new pyjamas, smiling, talking, and making the best out of a bad situation. Board games had been played, books read, and memories told. Songs had been sung, marshmallows toasted, and stockings hung. The rain had finally stopped, and the air was a lot milder than expected, offering its own Christmas gift. The sky was a deep blue that revealed no stars or flying reindeers but was magically charged by an atmosphere created from the excited energy of millions of children around the world.

Joey was sitting on her small-double bed, wrapped in a pale-green dressing gown and stripy green-and-white pyjamas. Fluffy cream socks covered her feet, and a chunky beige blanket snuggled around her hips.

Her grandmother and brother were downstairs in the living room, sipping Rémy Martin and playing poker with matchsticks, their usual Christmas Eve tradition.

Joey had gone to bed with a hug in a mug and a warm tingling sensation in her heart.

I wonder what my mum is doing right now? Maybe she has children to settle down. Nah! Ruby would have told me if Mum had kids. Besides, if she did go on to have more kids, they would probably be grown-ups by now. She might have grandkids to settle instead. She can't have. Ruby would have said. I'm sure she would know. I think she knows more about my mum's whereabouts than she lets on. My mum is snuggled down under her covers, warm and cosy and dreaming of the day she feels she can come home. You can come home, Mum. Anytime you like.

She stuck down the last piece of Santa wrapping paper over the long thin box in front of her and smiled warmly to herself.

A gentle tapping noise came from her bedroom door.

I bet that's Daisy. Too excited to sleep, no doubt.

'Come in,' she said quietly, not looking up.

'Hey,' said Josh, opening the door and poking his head around the frame.

Josh?

'What are you doing here? It's almost midnight.'

'Can I come in?' he asked, keeping his voice low.

She couldn't help the huge smile that was plastered all over her face. She waved him inside and watched as he closed the door and sat down on her bed. Amusement filled her eyes as she noticed the puffy Christmas pudding slippers on his feet.

'What are you wearing?'

He raised one leg in the air. 'Your gran made me take my shoes off and put on some slippers. Apparently, these were the only ones available, but I have my doubts.'

Ha! Gran's winding him up.

He flipped the footwear off. 'It's nice and warm in your house.'

'Oh, you're just here to pinch our warmth.'

He breathed out a laugh. 'No. I wanted to see in Christmas with you. It'll be here in five minutes.'

Joey felt elated. She had butterflies in her stomach, fairy dust in her heart, and floating love hearts circling her head.

She'd had quite a few, what she considered, magical moments with Josh Reynolds over time, but having him sit on her bed with her on Christmas Eve, waiting to see Christmas Day arrive, was officially her most favourite magical moment.

'I'm surprised Gran let you in.'

'I told her I'm on the wagon. Once she realised her brandy was safe, I was good to go.'

'I think she's already tipsy. You caught her off guard.'

'I was fully aware I was dealing with her drunk logic. Actually, she probably only talks to me because she was friends with my gran.'

Joey stayed tight-lipped about what her grandmother really thought of him. She lowered her hand once she realised she was twiddling her hair around her finger. She didn't want to look nervous. 'I was just wrapping your present.'

He stared down at her finger touching the gift, then revealed a present from behind his back that he had bought for her. 'I got you one too.'

Joey looked down at the ring-sized box in his hand.

Breathe, Jo. There is no way that's an engagement ring.

'Can I open it?'

He checked his watch. 'In a minute.'

Suddenly, time felt like it had stood still. Silence loomed whilst Joey stared desperately at her present like a child sitting around a Christmas tree.

Her dad used to place the presents all around her, tell her to take a deep breath, and then he'd shout, 'Go.' She would always unwrap all of her gifts before Nate, and her dad would hold her arm up triumphantly and say, 'Winner, winner, chicken dinner.' Nate would always point out the fact that they were having turkey that day, and her dad would laugh and play-fight with them in amongst the hoard of festive paper and cardboard boxes before leaving them alone to enjoy the presents that Santa had brought.

Joey looked away from Josh's gift.

It's not a ring. It's not a ring. Get a grip. Think of something else.

'Do you want to sleep here tonight, Josh?'

Her heart fluttered as his bright eyes smiled warmly at her.

I actually feel like crying right now. Look at him. The way he's looking at me. He's so beautiful. I love you so much. Be mine, Josh Reynolds. Stay with me forever.

'I'd love to,' he replied, 'but Jake and Anna want me with them Christmas morning. Anna's never had a family before, so it means a lot to her, and Jake would probably kill me if I let her down.'

Joey nodded and smiled.

Trumped by Anna Cooper. If it were anyone else, I probably would cry right now, for a different reason.

'But,' he added, 'I could stay for a couple of hours, if you like.'

I'll take it. I'll take you. Anytime. Oh, I'm so weak.

'I'd like that.'

He glanced over at her pillows. 'Do you want to get in bed now? I know you don't want me holding you, but a Christmas snuggle won't really count, will it?'

Joey laughed to herself. 'No, it doesn't count at Christmas.'

He removed his jeans and jumper and climbed in the bed and waited for her to slip under his arm.

Closing her eyes as her cheek touched his collarbone, she inhaled the fresh laundry scent embedded in his black tee-shirt and smiled. 'Is it time yet?'

He checked his watch. 'Almost.'

She snuggled closer to him, no longer caring about her rules or his. She wanted to be even closer to him. As close as she could possibly be. She lowered her head to rest upon his chest where she listened to his steady breathing. She wanted to fall asleep and wake up in the exact same hold.

This is us. This is right. This is perfect. I want to feel like this every moment of every day. Why can't he always be here with me? I miss him so much. Please don't cry. I don't want this to hurt. This moment is perfect. I won't let it hurt. I need to just embrace it and definitely not stroke his chest. Stop that. It's not helping matters.

'So,' he said quietly, 'what else were you up to tonight? Didn't fancy losing all your money at Casino Josephine downstairs?'

She could hear the smile in his voice. 'No. I was just thinking about my mum before you came in.' She felt him give her arm a little squeeze.

'You know, if you ever want to find her, I can help with that. I'll hire the best people, Jo.'

'Thanks, but sometimes I think I like her just being in my dreams.'

Josh tightened his hold on her, and she felt his mouth rest on her head.

'I wish you didn't have to go,' she said, slowly stroking his stomach with her fingertips.

'I wish that too,' he whispered into her hair.

I love you, Josh. I really want to tell you.

Josh adjusted his body in an attempt to sit up straight. He raised his arm away from her. 'It's time, Jo.'

She pulled herself off him and quickly handed over her gift. 'It's not much, I'm afraid. I didn't know you were going to be here.'

His eyes smiled directly into hers. 'I'll love it even if it's an empty box.'

Joey giggled. 'You're so soppy.'

Josh opened his present to see a silver tin with two artists' paintbrushes inside. They were thin-tipped with aubergine-coloured handles.

'I don't know if they're any good...'

'They're perfect. Thank you.' He handed her his present.

Joey steadied herself. She did not want to show any disappointment when she opened it to find a pair of earrings or whatever it was.

'Go on,' he urged.

She unwrapped the gold paper, thankful that her hands weren't shaking, and slowly lifted the lid off the dark-blue box that was inside.

That's not an engagement ring, but it is a ring.

A slow smile built on his face as she looked over at him.

'It's an eternity ring,' he said. 'People usually buy them for their first wedding anniversary. Well, that's what the jeweller told me. Obviously, that's not my reason. You've been my best friend since we were kids, so I kind of figured that you would continue to be my best friend for all eternity, so I wanted to get you something that represented that. It's platinum, and those little stones embedded all around it are sapphires. That's your birthstone.'

Joey stared down at the blue jewels. Her head felt a bit light and her voice had disappeared.

Josh cleared his throat and remained speaking quietly as though raising the volume would disturb the tranquillity between them. 'I want to make it very clear that this ring is by no means a friendship ring. It's an eternity ring. It's different. It's you and me for all eternity, if you'll have me hanging around that long.'

Joey wanted to cry, but a numbness was taking control of her emotions. She felt confused by the rapid combination of thoughts and feelings that had arrived all at the same time. It had rendered her speechless.

He leant forward and tenderly kissed her cheek. 'Merry Christmas, Joey.'

The touch jolted her out of her trance with the ring. A surge of warmth rushed through her body. She looked up at him, and it was only then that she realised that she had tears in her eyes.

'Hey,' he said softly, wiping away a falling teardrop.

She gazed at his chest, placing her hand over his heart, then she brought her face closer to his and kissed his lips.

13

Josh

The white candle in the pewter storm lamp sitting on the windowsill gave a warm glow to Josh's smiling face as he stood peering downhill from his bedroom view of Pepper Pot Farm in the distance. He could see the light from Joey's candle in her bedroom window. They had been lighting candles and putting them in their bedroom windows for each other since they were teenagers.

Josh hugged a blue hot water bottle to his chest. Anna had filled it for him from the water she had heated in a saucepan on the gas rings of their range cooker.

The electricity was still out all over Pepper Bay, but Josh felt warm inside even without heating.

It was two in the morning, and all he could think about was Joey's lips on his. He had secretly wanted to take their clothes off and slip down under the bed covers with her for the night, but she had pulled away from their kiss and simply said, 'Merry Christmas.'

Was that all it was, a Christmas kiss? It totally destroyed me. After her and her no-touching rule, she goes and kisses me. On the mouth. With such meaning. I know there was meaning behind that kiss. There had to be. It felt like it meant something, but she always feels that way. It's just her, I guess. If I left tomorrow, she wouldn't contact me. She never does. I'm not even her pen pal. This is so irritating. Why can't she just want me? I love her so much. At least she liked the ring. She looked a bit nervous for a moment. She probably thought I was going to propose. That's one way to end what we have. She likes things light. I have to keep to my boundaries like I've always done. I've never really given her much of a chance to fall in love with me anyway, but this time, I'm going to give her every chance. I'm not leaving. She'll see.

He felt the need to call his mentor but knew he had to deal with some things by himself. He was learning and growing, and he needed uncomfortable situations in order for him to make the necessary changes in his life. Rusty had taught him that, and Joey was good practice for him. His relationship with her was teaching him patience and making him think more before acting. He just wished that Joey could give him the love that he needed from her.

Oh God, that kiss. I wanted to... I could have just... I should have... I can't think about it. She took my breath away. She always takes my breath away. I could go back over there right now, wake her up, slip into bed with her, and... be back to square one with her. No. This has to stop. No more fling time. This is it this time. This is where I show her that there's more to me than a few weeks of fun. If I slip back into our old ways, nothing will ever change. I'm not doing that anymore. I have to focus. I have to get this right. It's not going to be easy if she kisses me again. Bloody hell, how did I hold back? Not sure if I should be patting myself on the back or slapping myself around the head. All I had to do was bring her back to me and we would have kissed again, and again, and again, and...

The bedroom door moved open a bit more and in trotted Max. He sleepily looked up at Josh standing there in his shorts and tee-shirt, then jumped up on the bed and settled himself at the end.

Josh climbed into bed and stared over at the already sleeping dog.

It's all right for some.

Jake poked his head around the doorway. 'You never could sleep on Christmas Eve.'

Josh laughed quietly. 'And what's your excuse?'

Jake walked in, wearing navy pyjama bottoms and a grey long-sleeved top. He stopped by the bed. 'I was just wondering where Max went.'

Josh rolled his eyes down at the dog.

Jake climbed into his brother's bed and pulled the cream brushed-cotton sheet and bright orange duvet up to his chest. 'It's cold in here.'

Josh glanced sideways at him. 'Jake, what are you doing?'

'Keeping warm,' he replied, trying to stretch his long legs without disturbing Max. 'Hey, you remember when Gran and Gramps used to sneak in our room and put presents at the foot of our beds?'

Josh warmed at the memory. 'Do you remember that year when they'd had a little too much Baileys, and they came in giggling and tripping over things? That was funny. I only pretended to stay asleep so they wouldn't feel disappointed.'

Jake grinned. 'Yeah, I got your sack of presents, and you got mine. Gran kept telling Gramps to be quiet, and they fell on the floor in a fit of muffled laughter.'

Josh laughed. 'Gramps was up a few hours later making a fry-up.'

'Yeah, no signs of a hangover for either of them.'

'I don't remember much about what Mum and Dad did for us.'

'Well, Mum would read you the story about Rudolph. That was your favourite, and she would put chocolate coins under our pillows, claiming the Tooth Fairy didn't mind because it was Christmas. She'd sing Silent Night to help

83

send us to sleep, but it never worked because we were far too excited. Mostly you, waiting for Santa to arrive.'

Josh held a weak smile. 'I've forgot a lot of things. What did Dad do?'

Jake's hesitation didn't go unnoticed.

'Jake?'

'Yes, erm, well, he didn't really do much, Josh. I think he felt that job was best left to Mum.'

'Do you think he was sad?'

Jake looked at him, then back across the room. 'I don't know.'

'I know he had depression. I've read what people said about him...'

'You know better than to believe what is written about our family. It's just tabloid gossip. They do it to all families like ours.'

'Do you think he caused the car accident that killed them?'

'I try not to think about it.'

Josh took a slow and steady breath. 'This will be our first Christmas on our own.'

Jake leaned over and nudged his arm with his own. 'We're not on our own. We've got each other, and we've got Anna now, not to mention that one down the end.'

'I always wanted a dog.'

'Well, you've got one now.'

Max stirred.

'You really love this woman, don't you, Jake?'

'Yep.'

Josh looked over at the candle flickering on his windowsill.

Jake followed his eyes. 'Are you going to tell Joey how you really feel about her this time, Josh?'

Josh started to twiddle his fingers. 'I don't want to ruin what we've got. She just wants to be friends, so I'm happy with that, for now. I also don't want to put any extra pressure on myself, but I am going to spend more time with her. I want to see if she can take me seriously.'

They both turned to stare silently over to the other side of the candle-lit, autumn-coloured room.

'Get some sleep now, Josh... or your presents won't magically appear at the bottom of your bed in the morning.'

Josh smiled to himself and snuggled down under his covers. He turned on his side so that he was facing the window.

Sweet dreams, Jo.

'Leave the door open on your way out, Jake, so that Max can come and go.'

'Okay.'

Josh realised that his brother wasn't moving. 'Anytime you like, Jake.'

Jake sniffed the cold air. 'I'm just going to sit here for a bit longer, if that's all right with you.'

Josh looked over his shoulder. 'You don't have to sit with me.'

'I'm not. I'm just warming myself before I have to make the cold walk back to my room. Besides, your sheets smell nice and fresh from where Anna changed your bedding last night. She really wants you to like her, Josh.'

'I do like her, Jake.'

'Go to sleep now.'

'Are you really just going to sit there?'

'Just five more minutes, then I'll be warm.'

Josh turned back to the window. He knew his brother was going to stay to make sure he fell asleep without any problems.

'I love you too, Jake.'

'Merry Christmas, Josh.'

* * *

Anna was the most excited out of everyone sitting on the rug in front of the crackling fireplace in Starlight Cottage on Christmas morning.

Josh laughed at the mound of presents beneath the Christmas tree. 'I think they're all for you, Anna.' He pulled another one out that had her name on it. 'It's from Santa.'

Anna giggled and turned to kiss Jake, who was sitting behind her with his legs wrapped around her. 'I have no idea where you hid this lot. I thought we said we were only buying each other one present.'

Jake gave a half-shrug. 'I lied.'

Anna pulled on the string and unwrapped the brown paper. She opened the box and pulled out a blue tin mug.

Josh frowned. 'Are you taking her camping?'

'He's being funny,' she told him. 'It matches my old tin kettle that I had when I was living in the tent on his roof.'

'I thought it was quite quaint, actually,' said Jake.

Anna grinned at Josh. 'You know he put foil-wrapped chocolate coins under my pillow. I found them this morning. Reckons the Tooth Fairy has a Christmas sister.'

Josh laughed. 'She visited me too.'

Anna pointed over at Max's bed. 'Even Max had doggy drops in his bed. The Christmas Fairy was very busy last night.'

Josh handed Anna his present. 'Here, have one from me. It's not as useful as your new coffee mug, but seeing as I only found out you existed five minutes ago, it's the best I could do.'

86

Anna unwrapped the brown paper to find a 5x8 white photo frame. She turned it over to see a portrait of her face drawn in pencil, with Jake and Josh either side of her, and Max next to Jake.

Josh wasn't sure what she was thinking, as she was just staring at it. 'I got a photo of you from Tessie, we all know how much she likes taking pictures, and I drew it from that. I know you've never had a family before, and we haven't had any photos done ourselves yet, so I thought it might be a good start...'

Anna silenced him by propelling herself forward and throwing her arms around his neck. 'I love it. Thank you so much, Josh.'

Josh struggled to breathe from Anna's tight hold. He lowered his head slightly as she pulled away and kissed his cheek. He watched her happily showing his artwork to Jake.

'He has always been the talented one,' said Jake, admiring the picture.

Josh laughed. 'And the better looking one.'

Anna giggled.

Jake handed her another present. 'Not sure any of my gifts are going to beat that now, but here you go. We still have a lot to get through.'

Anna opened her present to see star stud earrings made from white gold. 'More star jewellery for Starlight Cottage.' She smiled widely, said her thanks, and then jumped to her knees. 'I have a special one for Josh.'

She pulled over a big thin box.

'Is that what I think it is?' asked Jake.

Josh watched Anna nod. She had the widest grin and a sparkle in her ice-blue eyes.

'What's this then?' he asked.

'Open it and see,' she replied. 'It was gifted to me, and I thought I knew what I was going to do with it, but then I changed my mind, and then I met you and found out from Jake all about your artistic skills, so, it suddenly made sense.'

Josh took a breath as his eyes met with the oil painting of Starlight Cottage that Mr Blake, one of the previous owners of Anna's bookshop, had painted way back before the cottage had been renovated and extended by John Reynolds.

'Jake said that Edith always wanted this painting in her tea shop, but Betty Blake wouldn't sell it. She gave it to me though when she gave me the keys to the shop. She only let Jake buy the place because she knew it was for me,' said Anna. 'I was worried about the painting going in the tearoom in case someone flicked cake on it or something. It's yours now. You can decide.'

'Oh, wow. I don't know what to say.' Josh's eyes washed over the painting with admiration. He glanced over at his brother. 'What do you want me to do with it, Jake?'

Jake shrugged. 'You heard Anna. It's your choice.'

'Maybe I'll put it up in Gran's flat for now. I don't want anyone flicking cake on it either.'

Jake laughed. 'People don't tend to flick cake around the tearoom.'

'Thanks, Anna,' said Josh. 'This means a lot to our family.'

Anna smiled. 'I've also put aside all of the art supplies that were in the shop. We're updating the stock, so it's all yours, if you want it. You can come down to the shop one day next week and have a sort through.'

'Yeah, I'll take a look. Thanks a lot. I plan to stick around, and there's a lot I want to draw.'

Anna looked even happier than Jake. 'How long are you going to stay for?'

'I was thinking of buying a place here. Putting down roots.' He almost choked as Anna flung herself at his neck again.

'This is the best Christmas ever,' she said in his ear.

Max jumped on Josh and Anna, thinking it was playtime.

'It's not over yet, Anna,' said Jake. 'As soon as we've unwrapped this lot, it's cold showers all round, and then we need to go down to The Ugly Duckling to help make this a good Christmas for everyone.

Anna turned and pushed Jake down into the wrapping paper. 'The shower won't be too cold if we get in it together.'

Josh showed them both his palms. 'That's enough. I draw the line at showering with you two.'

Max jumped on him again and licked his face, making Jake and Anna laugh.

'That's your shower for today,' said Jake. 'And stop taking my shampoo.'

14

Joey

Joey was rinsing lettuce in the big stainless-steel sink in the kitchen inside The Ugly Duckling pub. Freddy was standing next to her, peeling potatoes whilst quietly singing "It's the Most Wonderful Time of the Year", and sounding almost as good as Andy Williams. The two back gas rings were alight, giving off some warmth to the room, and the old stone floor was completely dry beneath their chunky boots.

Thoughts of her dad singing whilst making the Christmas dinner filled her heart. Some years, she really missed her old life. She was a kid. Her dad was alive. She had no feelings for Josh Reynolds. Life was simple. The only plan she had for her future was which cartoon to watch that day on the telly. She'd put on her wellies. Splash around in the mud. Try to help her dad milk the cows and feed the chickens. She'd bake bread with her grandmother, and leisurely stroll around the farm with her black cat, Misty, following not far behind.

Stop thinking about Dad. You're going to end up crying into the salad.

'You know, you're such a good singer, Fred. You should go on one of those talent shows.'

Freddy wrinkled his nose. 'Nah, you're all right, Jo. I'm happy being a chef.'

Joey left her hands resting in the metal colander holding the lettuce. 'Wish I could sing.'

'You've got talent, Jo. You're a top baker. Get yourself on Bake Off or something.'

The loose bun at the back of her head bobbed slightly as she shook her head. 'I don't want to be on the telly. I don't think I would get on with being famous. Can you imagine what that is like. You can't even pop to the shops.'

'Yeah, nothing beats popping to the shops.'

Joey laughed and flicked water at him. 'Oh, hush.'

Freddy flinched. 'You can pack that in. It's cold enough, thanks.'

They went back to preparing the food. Freddy started singing again, this time quietly, and Joey thought he held a secret smile.

'Any news on you and Molly?' she asked. 'Or are you still failing miserably in that area?'

He held the potato peeler up in the air. 'There is no me and Molly. I'm not failing miserably at anything, thank you very much. What are you going on about?'

She turned back to her task. 'Just thought...'

'Thought wrong.'

'Okay. Sorry.' She paused. 'Not sorry, actually. I know you like her. Show her your ironing-board gut, that should do the trick.'

Freddy looked down at his stomach. 'Is that how easy you women are? All we have to do is whip off our tops?'

'You're ripped, Fred, with your protein shakes and your kale and quinoa salads. I'd show that off if it were me.'

'I would prefer my partner to adore me for my dazzling personality, if it's all the same.'

'But you don't have one of those, so you'll have to make do with flashing your body.'

'Bloody cheek! Well, what about you and Josh, eh?' Freddy waggled his eyebrows at her. 'Let's talk about that instead.'

Joey recoiled. 'Let's not.'

They went back to preparing Christmas dinner.

'Don't you like her at all, Fred?'

He huffed loudly just for dramatic effect.

Joey lowered her head into her shoulders as she bent further over the sink.

'She's a nice girl,' he said.

'You said that as though the words had been forced from your mouth.'

He raised his eyebrows. 'Well, they kind of were, Jo.'

'I'm merely passing the time.'

'No, you're not. You're being nosey. You're seeing if there's any room for you to interfere.'

Joey huffed. 'What's wrong with me wanting love for you, Fred? You should be grateful your friends take such a wide interest in your life.'

'Oh, is that a fact? Well, if you want to be so overly interested in my life, shall we start talking ingredients, recipes, and wholesale prices? Is any of that interesting enough for you? Hmm?'

'Oh, food shmood. I deal with that every day at work too, you know.'

'I prefer to keep my private life private, if you don't mind. Everything starts going wrong when you invite others into the mix.'

Joey's eyes gleamed with excitement. She raised her damp hands to arrange them in the shape of a heart in front of her chest. 'Does that mean there is something going on?'

He shot her a stern glare and threw a piece of potato peel at her head.

Joey turned off the dribbling tap and picked up the peel from the floor before he had a chance to go on about health and safety in the kitchen place. 'Shall we just go back to singing again instead?'

Freddy's face relaxed into a friendly smile. 'Go on then.'

They both belted out "Rockin' Around the Christmas Tree" whilst doing an out of sync jig at their allocated kitchen spots.

Freddy's mum, Ruby, walked in and placed down a ginormous cooked turkey that was covered in foil and wrapped in a few green tea towels. She immediately joined in with the singing and dancing.

Freddy gave his mum a twirl when she grabbed his arm.

Elaine entered the kitchen with Tessie.

Tessie dropped the black bin bags she was holding and immediately joined in with the partying.

Elaine reached into one of the bags and pulled out long strands of white and silver tinsel. She placed a piece around everyone's neck whilst singing in their flushed faces.

Freddy grabbed Joey and held her in his arms as they continued to sing and dance.

Anna sprinted into the kitchen with Jake, forcing him into a handheld dance, which made Joey laugh.

Jake was clearly making the effort for Anna's sake. Joey knew he wouldn't have danced otherwise. She was glad to see his serious side diminishing by the day.

The singing got louder, and the dancing turned into father-of-the-bride moves.

Joey's eyes caught Josh watching her from the doorway. He was leaning on the framework, with his arms folded and one foot hooked over the other. He smiled happily at her as the song came to a loud climax, making everyone cheer.

'Anna,' called over Elaine. 'Come on. I'll help you finish the tables.'

Jake and Anna followed Elaine and Tessie out of the kitchen.

Joey went over to Josh. 'What duty have you got?'

He started to twiddle with the silver tinsel draped down over her stomach. 'I haven't been assigned anything yet.'

Freddy waved him over. 'Peel some potatoes for me, mate. I'm just going to take Mum back up to Roseberry to pick up the stuffing she left behind.'

Ruby turned to face the turkey. 'Oh yeah. I knew I forgot something. For the life of me, I couldn't think what it was. I cooked Joey's stuffing as well. It smells so good, Jo.'

Joey smiled as Freddy led his mum out of the side door. She glanced sideways at Josh as he picked up the peeler. 'I also made some stuffing without any sausage meat so that you can have some too. I doublechecked all of my ingredients to make sure they were all vegan.'

'Thanks, Jo.'

She removed the tinsel and placed it on the counter on the other side of the room. 'We're only having chips and salad with the turkey and stuffing, but it'll be lovely.'

'I'm with my family and friends, that's all I need.' He glanced over at her hand.

She noticed he was looking at the ring he had bought her.

'You know you've got that on your wedding finger, right, Jo?'

I know.

She nodded. 'It only fits that finger.'

'People will think you're married. You won't get any dates.'

I'm pretending I'm married, if it's all the same to you. I'm your wife, and you don't even know it. Eternity, Josh. You said it. I'm going to live it.

'That's okay. I wasn't planning on dating anyone just yet anyway.' She caught Josh smiling to himself. 'Do you think you'll be ready to start dating again soon?'

You had better say no. Why did I even ask that?

She watched him shake his head slightly. 'I'm not interested in dating.'

'We can just hang out then, like we normally do, without having to worry about anyone else.'

'Just the two of us.'

'Are you going to start singing?'

Josh grinned widely. 'Nooo.'

Oh, sexy side smile is back. Bloody hell, Josh. Do you even know how good you look? I bet you practice that grin in the mirror. I can totally see you doing that.

Tessie popped her head into the kitchen. 'The floorboards are still a bit damp, but with all Anna's magical woodland theme going on out here, you don't really notice it anymore. We've put a few rugs down as well, so it's not too bad. That carpet was well and truly drowned though. Shame we couldn't save it, but hey ho. It's looking nice out here now. It feels as though pixies and imps are about to appear any minute.'

'That's great, Tess,' said Joey. 'As soon as Freddy gets back, he'll put the chips on and carve the turkey, and we're all set to go.'

Tessie's face lit up.

Nate peered over her shoulder. 'Come on you. There are bows and string to tie on chairs, and I'm making a right pig's ear of it.' He looked over at Joey. 'I did try, but apparently I lack skills in that area, so my daughters both told me. I'm on log duty instead, and I'm happy to report that the fire is doing nicely.'

Tessie laughed and pulled him away.

Josh looked back at Joey. 'It's nice how he calls Tessie's daughter his daughter as well.'

Joey raised one shoulder to her cheek. 'He's the only father she's known really, apart from Ed. The same goes for our Daisy. She looks at Tess as her mum. The four of them have always been close. Nate and Tessie raised those girls together after Henry died and Tori buggered off. Nate views them as his family. They're pretty tight. Have been for the last five years, I'd say. They're really close now. Took them long enough to rebuild their friendship after that bloody Dana Blake. I really hate that woman. Did you know, she forced her mum out of The Book Gallery and into that retirement village just so she could get her grubby little hands on her mum's money? Can you imagine where my family would be now if she did get away with selling our farm from under us. How on earth Nate ever got into bed with her is beyond me, especially when he had Tessie right there all the time. I wish he would get together with her.'

'Yeah, it's a shame they're not a couple.'

Joey nodded to herself. 'Some people just don't know what's right in front of them, do they?'

15

Josh

Josh kept rolling his eyes across the dinner table to look at Joey sitting opposite him. He loved how she was wearing the ring he bought her on her wedding finger. He was secretly pleased that other men would think she was taken and not ask her out. He didn't want anyone asking her out.

Every time I see that ring, I'm just going to pretend that you're my wife. If I visualise it enough and work towards making you realise I'm sticking around, I can manifest this dream into reality. I know what I want. I just have to believe in it. I have to believe in myself. No pressure. Just believe.

He glanced around at everyone enjoying their Christmas and was so happy he had decided to come back to Pepper Bay. He really missed his grandparents, but the warmth around him made him feel wanted and loved. He could always rely on Pepper Bay to make him feel better. He had a lifetime's worth of memories there. Plus, Joey Walker.

Josephine was trying to read Tessie's palm, and Nate was trying to get his grandmother to leave her alone. Tessie was laughing because Nate was getting the hump.

Daisy and Robyn were reading the jokes from the Christmas crackers, and Elaine and Ed were laughing merrily along with the girls' giggles.

Freddy was adjusting Ruby's pink paper hat, as it kept falling down to sit upon the bridge of her glasses. In the end, she pushed her glasses up to her head and her problem was solved.

Jake and Anna were showing Joey pictures on Jake's phone of Anna's friend, Stan, volunteering for Crisis in London, and Max and the Walkers' shaggy black-and-grey dog, Scruff, were sleeping on a dry navy rug by the fireplace.

Josh took a slow and steady breath. He felt peaceful in amongst the lively chatter. He saw his brother glance over at him and smile.

Jake looks so content. This life really suits him. I'm glad he's happy.

Freddy nudged his elbow. 'You all right, Josh. You want me to help you with your hat?'

Josh laughed. He rolled his eyes up to see the brim of his green paper hat. 'I'm good, thanks.'

Freddy raised his glass of champagne to clink glasses with Josh's glass of lime water. 'The fridge hasn't been opened all night, so the desserts should be fine. Got some of Nate's cheese in there too. I know you can't eat that, but there are some grapes and apples to go with the crackers, if you fancy that.'

Got to admit, I really do miss the cheese from Pepper Pot Farm.

'Actually,' said Josh, standing up. 'I have an announcement to make.'

Josephine fluttered her wrinkly old eyelids. 'You've proposed to our Joey. That's why she's wearing that ring.'

Joey looked distraught and quickly placed her hand on her lap under the table.

'Gran!' she snapped.

'Erm, no,' said Josh, feeling some heat hit his cheeks.

Oh my God, her face. Just the thought of me proposing to her clearly horrified her.

Jake stood up. 'Josh and I have arranged a little surprise for everyone.'

Tessie clapped her hands quietly. 'Ooh, what is it?'

'We have a friend who lives in Poole who owns a rather nice yacht, and it happens to be waiting for us in the bay. We thought you might like to have dessert on board the Sarah-Ellen.'

'How wonderful,' said Elaine. 'Come on then, everyone. What are we waiting for?'

'Bring your coats,' said Jake. 'The inside will be warm, but if anyone wants to stand on the deck, it might be a bit chilly.'

Ed was the last to leave the pub. He locked the door and followed everyone down to the small shingle beach.

A white speedboat was waiting to transport its passengers over to the large yacht waiting for them in the near distance.

'Ooh, look at that,' said Tessie, pointing out to sea.

Everyone took turns to walk along a slimy, narrow walkway that led to the small boat. They had to wait their turn, as the speedboat didn't fit them all in at the same time.

Josh waited till last, watching the smiles build on each face that passed him to get to the boat. He laughed to himself when Nate carried Tessie, then smiled warmly when he saw his brother do the same thing for Anna. He glanced at Joey as she made her own way across the concrete lump in the sea. She was carrying Scruff, who was clearly afraid of the water. The dog was squirming in her arms, making her trip to the speedboat a struggle.

Freddy helped Josephine and his mum into the boat, then made a grab for Joey and Scruff.

Daisy and Robyn were laughing at Elaine as Ed pretended to throw her into the sea.

Josh looked down at Max once everyone had left. 'I guess it's just you and me, mate.'

Max made a huffing sound, which made Josh laugh.

The ride over to the yacht was quick, and Josh had no problem putting Max onto the small platform at the back of the boat.

A staff member immediately fitted the golden retriever with a life jacket as Josh stepped onto the vessel.

The warmth hit him as soon as he stepped inside. Music was already playing, and everyone was gathered around a long table lined with desserts.

'This boat is lovely,' said Elaine, brushing past him.

Josh smiled and nodded.

'Look at this, love,' said Ed, leading Elaine away. 'It's got a mini ice machine behind the bar.'

Tessie leaned over behind Josh to stroke the cream leather seating. 'This is a bit posh, eh, Josh?'

'I like it,' said Ruby. 'It's got a light and airy look about it, and I like how the wood shines.'

'Yeah,' said Tessie. 'It's definitely polished in here.'

'This belongs to your friend, does it, Josh?' asked Ruby.

Josh nodded. 'Yeah. He was happy to let us have her for the night.'

Ruby smiled. 'Ooh, what a lovely man.'

Josh saw Jake lead Anna outside to the front deck. His eyes scanned the cabin for Joey, but he couldn't see her.

She must be in the bathroom.

Robyn and Daisy distracted him. 'Can we go downstairs, Josh?'

'Sure. There's a small games room down there somewhere. Look around, and ask a member of staff if you need any help with anything.'

'Thanks,' said Daisy.

Josh gave a slight nod behind the girls. 'Or you could ask that man over there in the black suit.'

'Who is he?' asked Robyn.

The corners of Josh's mouth curled. 'Let's just call him your guardian angel.'

'You mean he's our babysitter,' said Robyn. She glanced at Daisy and shook her head.

Daisy shrugged. 'I don't mind.'

'Do we have to wear these life jackets?' asked Robyn. 'No one else is.'

Josh nodded sympathetically. 'Yeah, sorry.'

The girls walked away, mumbling about the safety rules thrust upon them by Jake.

Josh headed for the door that led to outside. He leant on the frame and watched his brother slow-dancing with Anna at the front of the boat. The polished deck gleamed under a row of white lightbulbs hanging above them.

He had never seen his brother look so peaceful before. A twinge of jealously hit him. He wanted to feel that way too. He longed to hold the girl he loved in his arms and slow-dance his way towards tranquillity.

A warm smile built on his face as Jake and Anna kissed tenderly. He sighed deeply as they walked away around the side of the boat, oblivious to his presence. He stepped forward into the evening and went over to the edge where white lights lit the water from beneath the vessel. He stared absentmindedly into the sea.

'Hey,' said a soft voice behind him.

Josh smiled to himself at the impact her voice had on him. He could feel the hairs on the back of his neck tingle as he raised his head to see her appear at his side.

'Are you having a nice time, Jo?'

'I don't think I'll ever forget this Christmas.'

They both looked down into the illuminated sea. A comfortable silence filled the cool air.

Joey released a slow breath. 'It's absolutely beautiful here.'

Josh turned to face her. His bright eyes were mesmerised by the gentle lighting twinkling in her taupe eyes. The cool air washed across her cheeks, giving them a fresh pink flush.

'You staring at me?'

I could look at you forever. You're beautiful, Jo.

'Would you like to dance?' he asked softly.

She turned and held out her arms, and he placed one arm around her waist and moved his other to find her hand.

Her body automatically gravitated closer towards his, and he closed his eyes as he lowered his head so that their faces touched. They gently swayed to the soft sound of Ray Charles singing "You Don't Know Me", which was drifting out from the opened doorway of the cabin.

Joey moved their linked fingers up towards his chest and gently stroked his back with her other hand.

The smell of the salty, night-time air was overruled by Joey's sweet lemony scent. Josh breathed her in as his cheek slowly brushed against hers.

God, this woman. I can't hold back much longer. I can feel the oxygen leaving my brain. She needs to stop stroking my back. She feels so good. Everything feels so perfect.

Joey's hand slowly moved up his spine and curled around the back of his neck. He opened his eyes as her fingertips reached into his hair.

Their faces moved apart a touch, and their heads slowly turned until their lips lightly traced over each other's.

'I love you, Jo,' he whispered.

'I love you too.'

'You're my best friend.'

She moved her face and pulled her body back. She smiled, but it looked weak. 'I'm going back inside. It's getting cold.'

He felt his heart sink as her arms slipped away from his hold.

Why did I say that? What an idiot. Now she thinks I was just saying I love you like a friend. Talk about ruin the moment, Josh. Great! Bloody fantastic.

Max trotted over and licked him on the hand.

Josh stared glumly down at the dog. 'Did you hear what I said to her, mate?'

Max sneezed, making it look like a nod.

16

Joey

The week between Christmas Day and New Year's Eve had been completely occupied by all of the repairs that needed doing in Pepper Lane. New floorboards and carpet had been laid. Damaged stock and furniture had been replaced. Homes and businesses had been aired, repainted, and thoroughly cleaned of all toxins, waste, and damp patches. The electricity had finally come back on early Boxing Day morning. A spokesperson for the council had arrived in Pepper Bay, called the residents to a meeting in The Ugly Duckling, and happily reported that work on the riverbank was going to start on January 2nd. Josephine had shouted out, 'About bloody time.' The rest of the meeting had gone by without any more heckling.

Joey kept herself busy in Edith's Tearoom. Once the flooring was sorted, she had repainted all of the skirting and managed to save the tables by sanding the wooden feet and varnishing the tips.

Everyone had insurance, but Jake had paid for everything to get fixed as soon as possible so that Pepper Lane could get back to normal without everyone worrying too much. Workers had been paid triple time to come over from Sandly and places further afield to help with the work that needed doing.

Josh had stayed away from the tea shop and Joey. They hadn't spoken since saying goodnight on Christmas. He had been staying up at Starlight Cottage.

Joey wasn't entirely sure if she was pleased. On one hand, she felt as though she could breathe again, and she didn't want to see him because it was getting too hard. On the other hand, she rolled back tears every night whilst staring up at the candle in his window burning just for her. She missed him so much, and that felt even harder. When he had told her that he loved her on the yacht, she had taken it the wrong way, and she had felt foolish ever since. She really thought he was telling her that he was in love with her, but his best friend line clinched the deal. She finally knew where she stood. He genuinely loved her as a friend. She didn't even have the strength in her to cry herself to sleep on that night.

The new year was almost upon her, and she was looking forward to it being a good one. The local estate agent, Wendall James, had promised to let her know as soon as Honeybee Cottage came on the market, and Joey knew that Loretta was going to move out in January, as she had told her so herself. Joey could barely contain her excitement whenever she thought about living in her dream home.

She had been saving up for years to buy her own place, and she desperately wanted a cottage on Pepper Lane. Honeybee Cottage was her favourite. It was the most modern, built around thirty years ago after the original cottage was in too much disrepair to be saved, and it was the closest to the shops. It was perfect for her in every way. She couldn't wait to move in. She already had big ideas for the place.

'Rubes, I'm just going to take Anna over a coffee and a cupcake.'

Ruby popped her head out of the kitchen door. 'Take your time. I'm just reorganising the bottom cupboards.'

Joey poured some coffee into a takeaway cup and placed a vanilla cupcake topped with a light swirl of chocolate buttercream into a small box. She made her way up the slope towards The Book Gallery.

Josh sitting on the newly sanded wooden floor inside the bookshop wasn't what she was expecting to see as she entered. She felt her legs turn to jelly and then instantly freeze in the doorway. Her heart started to gallop in her chest.

Josh. You're here. I really want to give you a hug. I've missed you so much. Oh God, it's taking every inch of strength I have not to throw myself at you. Oh, it hurts. It really hurts. Come on, Jo, breathe.

Azure-blue eyes rolled up to greet her. 'Hey, Jo.'

Joey stared at him until her brain reminded her why she was there. 'I brought Anna a coffee and a cupcake.'

'She's upstairs in the flat.'

Joey inhaled the smell of fresh paint as she entered the shop. She glanced down at the mass of art equipment surrounding him on the floor. 'What are you up to?'

'Sorting this lot. New stock is due soon, so Anna wanted me to see if anything Betty Blake left behind was any good.'

'I've not seen… You've not been… I've not seen you for a few days.'

Josh tipped his head towards the window. 'I've been around. Mostly in the cellar with Ed, helping to get things straight. I learnt a few new things I never knew I could do. Ed does make me laugh. He never changes, does he? He still reminds me of a pirate. I don't think he'll ever change his look.'

She stared glumly at the coffee cup as Josh laughed to himself. 'You haven't been in the tearoom.'

He rolled a paintbrush back and forward in front of him. 'I looked in from time to time. You were busy with repairs.'

'I would have still made time for… to make you a cup of tea.'

He smiled at the floor. 'I didn't want to bother you, Jo.'

You can bother me anytime. I don't mind. I wish I'd seen you. I wouldn't have felt so lonely these past few days if I knew you were still so close to me. Just a wave would have meant so much. I guess I should be grateful you still lit a candle for me to see. I just wanted more, that's all. I want more right now.

Joey looked to the back of the shop. 'Is Jake up there with Anna? I don't want to walk in on them smooching.'

Josh laughed as he looked up at her. 'I know, right. I feel as though I'm living with a couple on their honeymoon. Every time I turn around, they're kissing or hugging or looking dreamily at each other. It's like being trapped in a romance novel.'

What would you know about romance. You just have sex. Oh, shut up, Jo. Where the hell did that just come from? I know exactly where it came from. I want some of my own romance, and with him. Anna and Jake are so lucky. I want a normal relationship likes theirs. I want to be able to kiss Josh whenever I want, like right now, for instance.

'So, is Jake up there?'

'Oh, no. He's walking Max.'

She carefully stepped her shaky limbs over his legs and the art equipment and headed towards the internal stairs.

'Will you be in the pub tonight for New Year's?' he called out.

She paused at the door. 'Yeah, I'll be there. Will you?'

'Yeah. I'll see you tonight. Elaine's getting out the karaoke machine. We'll have to do a song like we normally do. Are you up for that?'

Great! Let's just pretend everything is normal between us.

'Okay,' she said, trying her best to sound cheerful.

She glumly made her way up the bare stairs. Her shoulders felt lead-heavy, and her legs decided to join in. She entered the flat to meet with Anna's smiley face.

'Hello, Jo. Excuse the mess. I don't know where to put everything. I'll be glad when we can shift this lot downstairs.'

Joey was surrounded by books, boxes, paintings, and black bin bags that were full to the brim with old soft furnishings.

Anna flapped her hand out to her side. 'All of Betty's old furniture went yesterday. It was so sad seeing her life packed up like that and taken away to the rubbish tip. I found a box of her jewellery. Her daughter's coming to collect it in a couple of days.'

'I guess she didn't need to take much moving to a retirement village.'

'It's all your things though.'

'My mum's things are still in our loft.' Joey placed the coffee cup and cupcake box down upon a stack of large brown boxes.

'I hardly own anything,' said Anna, not looking too fussed about that. 'Jake keeps buying me clothes and asking if I need anything else, but I guess I've always been a light traveller. Is that coffee for me?'

Joey nodded. 'Yes, and a cupcake.'

'Ooh, lovely. Thanks very much.' She pointed to a floor space. 'Sit here with me for a bit.'

Joey joined Anna on the dusty floorboards.

Anna giggled. 'You won't notice the dust in a minute.'

Joey smiled. 'How are you getting on, Anna? You haven't been here long. Do you feel settled yet?'

Anna removed the lid from her cup and blew into the dark liquid. 'Hmm, I love it here. Feels like home already.' She smiled over at Joey. 'I never knew what home actually felt like until I met Jake. He's my home.'

Joey felt her heart warm. 'Aww, that's lovely, Anna.'

Anna nodded towards the door. She kept her voice low as she asked, 'What's happening with you and Josh?'

Joey wrinkled her nose and shook her head slightly. 'We're just friends.'

Anna raised her eyebrows. 'Well, from an outsider's point of view, you look more than just friends.'

'We've got a lot of history, that's all.'

Anna quietly sipped her drink. Her eyes rolled down to Joey's wedding finger and grinned.

Joey touched her ring. 'We're just friends, Anna.'

Freddy's right. I shouldn't let anyone know how I feel about someone. Might be a bit late for that though. Seems like everyone in Pepper Bay knows I love Josh. Well, they assume. He just doesn't assume. Maybe it's time I did say something to him and be done with the consequences. I've got to stop being a coward. What would I lose? What would I gain? I should have more self-respect. He hasn't spoken to me in days, and just now he said we'll sing together tonight at the pub, and I just said, okay, like a right idiot. Why is it so hard to have some bloody willpower? Why is it so hard to take my own advice?

Anna mumbled something into her coffee, regaining Joey's attention.

'Did you just say that Josh is insanely ripped?'

Anna shrugged. 'Well, he is, and that's what you're missing out on.'

That's all I need, thinking about his hot body. God, that man is sexy. We've fitted in a lot of great sex during our summer holidays over the years. I love how we are together. Don't think I've ever felt embarrassed to show him my body. Not that anyone else has ever seen it. Maybe that's my problem. I need to sleep with more men. I really do not want to sleep with anyone but Josh. He's slept with other people. I wish he hadn't. Why did he have to go and do that? Why couldn't he just be mine like I'm just his? He did say he was a drunken blur back then. I know he wasn't drunk with me. Well, there was the odd occasion where we were both drunk.

'You're not allowed to think about Josh that way, Anna. He'll be your brother-in-law soon.'

Anna giggled. 'Do you think Jake will marry me one day?'

'Definitely. That man is in serious love with you. Any fool can see that.'

'Funny that. That's what we say about Josh with you.'

'If Josh Reynolds was in serious love with me, Anna, I'm pretty sure he would have told me by now.'

'Actions speak louder than words.'

'Any particular actions you are thinking of?'

Anna tipped her head down at the eternity ring. 'That's one.'

17

Josh

Bill Haley's "Rock Around the Clock" died a thousand deaths in Pepper Bay, thanks to Josh and Joey's karaoke attempt that was mostly out of tune because of Joey. Josh laughing his way through half the song did little to help matters. Everyone in The Ugly Duckling gave them a big cheer as soon as they finished, and Josh secretly suspected it was because they had finally finished murdering the tune.

Freddy got up next and flawlessly belted out Elvis Presley's "Jailhouse Rock".

'That was so funny,' said Josh, tugging Joey's arm as they neared the bar.

'That's one word for it,' said Nate, grinning at his little sister.

Tessie nudged him. 'Hey, I'd like to see you sing one day. You never go up there.'

Nate laughed. 'I'll go after Jake.'

All eyes turned to Jake.

Anna patted his chest with the hand she had resting there. 'Go on, Jake. You'll have fun.'

Jake's serious face pretty much told everyone that he would never in a million years have fun singing karaoke.

Anna giggled at him and kissed his cheek, softening his hostile glare towards Nate.

'No one's got time anyway,' said Tessie, checking the white clock on the wall. It's almost midnight. As soon as Fred is done, we'll be doing the countdown.'

Josh turned to Joey. 'Come outside, quickly.' He tugged her arm, and she followed him out to the beer garden.

'Josh, it's freezing out here.'

He pulled her into his strong arms. 'Yeah, but look how sparkly it looks.'

Joey raised her brow. 'Sparkly?'

Josh looked around at the fairy lights and Victorian street lamps. He smiled widely as the snow machine attached to the roof started to blow fake snow down upon their heads. He pulled her over to a wooden table and sat down on its edge, with Joey resting between his legs.

'Hey, how do you feel about me sticking around for a lot longer?' he asked quietly.

Joey blew some fake snow from her lips and blinked away some more. 'How long for?'

'Oh, I don't know. Forever.'

He watched her eyes widen.

'Really?'

He tightened his legs around her as his arms pulled her closer towards his chest. 'I wanted to run it by you.'

'Why?'

'Because we talk about everything.'

The corners of her mouth twitched. 'No, we don't. We hardly know each other, really. I only see you once or twice a year for a few weeks. There are probably loads of things we don't know about each other.'

I feel I know you, and I know I always show you the real me.

Josh gave a half-shrug. 'All the more reason to stick around.' He lifted her hand and stroked her ring. 'Eternity, Jo.'

The countdown to the new year was the only sound around them.

112

He felt her body jolt slightly as everyone inside the pub shouted out, 'Happy New Year.'

'Happy New Year,' she whispered.

He stood up and cupped her face in his hands. 'Happy New Year, Jo.' Before she had a chance to walk away, he kissed her.

A rush of heated adrenaline filled him from head to toe. Her lips felt soft and warm, and her tongue fed his desire for her even more. Her hands reached into his hair, gripping him, and his clasp on her face tightened as he tried to pull her even closer, even though there wasn't any space left between them. Their faces were flushed and their breathing heavy as their bodies locked.

'Josh.' Her trembling voice vibrated on his lips.

'Jo.' He tried to add more but the fake snow fell into the crack between their mouths as their lips loosened. He kissed her again but had to stop and raise his hand to remove a piece of snow that had joined their mouths. He felt her lips curl into a smile on his.

'Bloody snow.'

Joey breathed out a laugh. 'It's getting everywhere.'

He lowered his hands and sat back on the table. 'Look, Jo, I'm sorry about the kiss. I know we have rules about this touching business, but everyone deserves a New Year's Eve kiss.'

She frowned at him. 'I'm not sure if you deserved one.'

Josh's face was awash with amusement. 'Why? What did I do?'

'I don't know yet. I'll think of something.'

He laughed at her and reached out to tuck away a strand of her golden hair. His breath caught as she moved her face into his palm and closed her eyes.

'What are you hoping this year will bring you, Josh?'

You.

He tried not to show his disappointment when she moved her face away from his hold.

He shrugged as her eyes opened and sleepily looked his way. 'Peace. Fresh start. New life.'

'And you think you'll get that here in Pepper Bay?'

He nodded. 'Hope so. This place has always felt like home, thanks to Gran. Jake's happy here. I want to be too.'

Joey shivered.

Josh quickly stood and wrapped her in his arms, rubbing her back as she lowered her head to his shoulder. He stared over at the jam jars filled with fake candles lining the pathways as the snow continued to drift down.

Elaine had tried to make the beer garden look as magical as possible for Christmas, and she had done a great job, especially after a lot of it had been washed away in the flood.

Josh knew they would both be warmer inside the pub, but he didn't want to share any more of the night with anyone else. He also didn't want to let Joey go. He gently kissed the top of her head.

'Do you want me to stay in Pepper Bay, Jo?' he whispered into her hair.

He felt her muffled voice vibrate into his top. 'Yes.'

Yes! This is such a good start. She's letting me hold her. I just kissed her. She wants me to stay. We haven't had sex. I think I might be growing on her. She might just warm to having a proper partner. I reckon I can win her heart. As long as I don't sleep with her, I'm making progress.

His arms tightened around her. He really wished their bodies were as close as they could be.

'Will you walk me home, Josh? I'm tired, and I've had too much wine.'

'Sure. Let's get your coat and say our goodbyes.'

She slipped out of his hold and went back into the pub.

He removed some fake snow from his eyelash and followed her inside.

It took a lot longer to leave the pub than he had expected, as everyone kept kissing them and yelling out *Happy New Year* every five minutes.

Josh deeply inhaled the cold night air as he finally got to step outside onto Pepper Lane. 'Bloody hell, I thought we'd never get out of there.'

Joey laughed and placed her arm around his waist, slouching her head down. 'Drunk people.'

He led the way across the road, looking over at Edith's Tearoom. 'Shall we spend the night in the flat?'

'Are you sure? I don't want to breathe stale alcohol breath on you. It's not fair of me. That's it, I'm going to give up drinking just for you.'

Josh smiled and helped her keep her balance as her ankle wobbled over the conduit. 'That's very nice of you. I think I'll survive your boozy breath tonight. What I don't think I'll survive is getting you all the way back up to Pepper Pot Farm.'

Joey patted her grey cloth handbag. 'I have the keys to the shop.'

He held her hand as they headed down the slope towards the tea shop. He waited quietly as she fumbled with the keys, and when he realised they would probably end up on the street for the night, he took over and opened the door to let them in.

'Ooh, it's cold in here,' she said, watching him lock the door behind them and sort out the alarm.

Josh followed her up to the flat, making sure she didn't take a tumble on the stairs. 'I'll put the heating on low for the night.'

She glanced over at the bedroom. 'Leave it off, Josh. We're getting in bed now. We'll soon be warm.'

Josh did as he was told and followed her into the spare room. 'You want to sleep in this room tonight?'

She nodded and quietly got undressed down to her underwear. She turned to the pine wardrobe and pulled out an oversized white tee-shirt that had *I Feel Pretty* written on it in bold red letters and quickly slipped it on. She struggled to unfasten her bra and remove it through her sleeve, so Josh stepped forward to help. She bent down to the bed and climbed down under the covers.

'It's cold in here.'

Her voice brought him out of his trance-like state. He stopped staring at her white bra in his hand and stripped off to his grey boxers. 'I'll just bring in the plastic bowl and a bottle of water for you, just in case you feel sick in the night.'

He quickly headed for the kitchen and returned within seconds. He placed the grey bowl on the floor by her side, then he broke the seal on the bottle and put the still mineral water on the bedside cabinet.

Her arm met his shoulder as soon as he was at her side. She snuggled her body close to his and rested her head on his chest.

He gently stroked her hair whilst staring up at the dull ceiling. All inspiration, aspiration, and motivation hadn't even had the courtesy of fading away. They just left him, right there and then. He felt the need to protest, but he lacked the energy to bicker with himself. He just wanted to have a normal relationship, but watching her get changed and snuggle up to him in bed only reminded him once again that he did not have that at all.

Josh had seen Joey naked plenty of times. He knew every inch of her body. He had watched her get changed before and had held her in bed many times, but tonight something had just felt weird. He felt numb. His breathing was shallow, his emotions were still, and his mind was in a daze. He couldn't quite put his finger on what exactly it was that he was feeling. He just knew he didn't like it. He could feel a thin line of sweat on his brow.

I need to focus on my breathing. Slow and steady. Nice and easy. Everything is fine. I'm just over-wanting things, that's all. Too much pressure. I need to visualise and be grateful, not want and suffer for those wants. I want to call Rusty, but I can't while Joey's awake. Her breathing hasn't settled yet. I'll wait till she's nodded off, then I'll call him. I wish my mojo would give me some sort of warning if it's going to bugger off. I just have to channel my energy. I went off road for a moment. Can't be helped. Happens to everyone. I lost my concentration. I feel like crap now. I won't be able to sleep till I've spoken to Rusty. Not now. Why is it that I can figure out the reason, see the logic, and know what I have done wrong, but still the crappy feeling won't disappear? How the hell does that work exactly?

He closed his eyes and listened to the silence whilst waiting for Joey to drift off.

She tilted her head and gently kissed his collarbone. 'Night, bestie.'

The stress in him effortlessly changed to sadness.

* * *

'What time is it there?' asked Rusty. His voice held a soft Scottish tone.

Josh automatically moved his face away from his phone to glance at the small silver carriage clock sitting on top of the windowsill behind him. He turned back to face the

117

kitchen and snuggled further into his grandmother's comfy cream chair. He tugged his dark-green dressing gown closer to his chest. 'Just gone one.'

'So, you're already in the new year. What's it like so far?'

Josh scrunched his tired eyes. 'Still no flying cars.' He listened to Rusty's muffled laugh. 'Seems funny we're in different years.'

'New York will catch up soon enough. You having trouble sleeping, Josh?'

Josh sighed quietly. 'Just felt a little low.'

'How long have you been feeling like that?'

His soothing voice lifted Josh's head above the water, stabilising his breathing.

'Not long. I've had a good night, mostly. There was a moment where I wanted a drink, but it passed. I was ready for bed tonight when I suddenly felt down. It just came over me.'

He visualised Rusty sitting by the window, staring out at the view of the park below him. It was somewhere he had also sat many times. He would imagine he could see Pepper Pot Farm in the distance, and Joey walking across the field. He glanced over at the bedroom where she was sleeping.

Rusty's voice interrupted his thoughts. 'Have you been putting pressure on yourself?'

Josh gave a slight nod. 'Yeah.'

'Try to remember the plan you set yourself before you arrived in Pepper Bay.'

Josh sniffed back the cold air. 'I know. I came off track. It's hard sometimes.'

'I know.'

'I wish you were here. I wouldn't mess up if you were with me,' said Josh quietly, the words catching in his throat.

'You have to mess up in life, Josh, otherwise, what would you learn? It's okay, you know. No one is perfect. We all have ups and downs. What matters is we try again. You're going to have a good sleep, and when you wake up, you will start again. We often fall on our journey because the pathway is sometimes bumpy, but we must always get back up and continue to move forward. That's the important part.'

Josh nodded to himself. 'It was just a bump in the road. I tripped.'

'That's right.'

'I'm not going to dwell on it.'

'Good.'

'Thanks, Rusty.'

'I didn't do anything.'

Josh smiled warmly. 'Yeah, you did. You reminded me to stay focused.'

18

Joey

Joey woke to an empty bed and a semi-hot mug of tea waiting for her on the pine bedside cabinet. Her hand reached out from beneath the quilt for the drink. She could feel that the central heating had been switched on. Her body felt warm and cosy, but her mouth felt like cardboard, and her head held a dull ache. She never was much of a drinker, but the alcohol was flowing thick and fast on New Year's Eve. Every time she finished her drink, another was placed in her hand, and she had decided to hell with it.

Her bleary eyes peered at the old twin-bell alarm clock that had the ability to wake the dead. She could do with another couple of hours, which was so unlike her.

I am never drinking that much again. In fact, New Year's resolution number one. No more booze. Ever. Solidarity for Josh, and my head.

She groaned as she tipped her head to sip the tea. She flopped back to the pillow and held the brown mug on her chest.

Resolution number two. Make a start on those lollies. I keep putting it off. I've got to get motivated. My own brand of lollipops for the shop is definitely happening this year. No more putting things off. Step one, get up. Step two, shower. Step three, paracetamol. Step four, breakfast. Step five, boil sugar. Only if head is clear by then. Okay. I have a plan. I have a day.

She started to feel better already.

A nice quiet day in the shop. Oh wait, Josh. Where is he?
Resolution number three. Stop touching Josh Reynolds. Why
can't I stop touching him? It's driving me nuts. I really need
to stick to the plan. I can't keep breaking my own rule. Oh,
this is so hard. How many times have I touched him already?
When he first got here, that was one. By the shop door, that
was two. Oh God, and I kissed him. What is wrong with me?
Why can't I do this? I can do this. You're doing this, Jo. This
is well and truly getting done. New year, new start. I, Joey
Walker of Pepper Pot Farm, do solemnly swear that I'll not
touch Joshua Reynolds of London ever again. This is going
to be my year. It's going to be a good year. A great year.
Goodbye, old me. Hello, new me. I can do this. I can totally
do this. Right. Let's get up. Today is a good day.

* * *

Joey was having a slouchy day. She was wearing her slouchy
indoor clothes, which consisted of a pink tracksuit and cream
slippers. Her hair was pulled back and slouched loosely
almost at the top of her head. She was slouched over the
oven, concentrating on the long thermometer sticking out of
a large metal pan. She turned to glance at her notebook to
doublecheck the bubbling sugary liquid was the correct
temperature.

Edith's Tearoom was closed for the day. As much as Joey
loved to have customers, she also loved the quiet days for
using the kitchen at her own leisure. She loved being by
herself, in her own head, creating recipes or simply baking.
The whole process, from weighing ingredients to opening
the oven door to allow the freshly baked aroma to fill the
room, made her calm and relaxed. It kept her mind occupied

and soothed her aching heart whenever it reminded her it was hurting.

The back door opened, making her jump. She looked over to see Josh walk in, wearing his own tracksuit.

He quickly closed the door, blocking out the icy air.

She gazed at his glossy forehead. 'Have you been jogging?'

His grinning face was fresh with a slight pink flush and a bit of a red nose. 'Yeah. I went with Jake.'

She watched him drink water from the faucet and cuff his mouth on his sleeve. She smiled warmly to herself. He always drank straight from the tap, and his grandmother would tell him off, even when he was an adult. It always made Joey laugh, especially when Edith would try to wipe Josh's mouth with her hankie and he would duck out of her way.

'I am so not as fit as Jake,' he said breathlessly. 'I think he was trying to kill me. What are you up to? What's in the pot?'

She moved him a step back as his face came too close to the sticky mixture. 'Mind yourself. Hot sugar on the skin is no fun.'

'What are you making?'

Joey edged away from his sweaty body. 'I'm going to start selling my own brand of lollipops.'

She examined his face for any signs of amusement, but he looked genuinely interested.

'Ooh, what flavours?'

'I'm going to try dandelion first. See how I go.'

She fell back onto her heel as he leant forward and kissed her head.

'Good luck. Whatever you make will be great. I'm off for a quick shower. I need to defrost. I swear, I can't feel my face.'

Her eyes followed him all the way to the door.

Let the record state that I did not touch him. He kissed me. That was out of my control, and therefore does not count. I have not broken my rule.

She glanced back at the pot.

I have, however, just burnt my bloody syrup. Argh!

She picked up the pot and placed it down into a bowl of icy water.

That's it. I've had enough. I should have had my breakfast first anyway. I just need to concentrate, and I can't do that with a rumbling tummy. A sexy, sweaty Josh did little to help matters as well. God, I love his sweaty look. What am I doing? Don't think about that look.

She switched the oven off and headed back up to the flat for a bowl of bran flakes with a sliced banana.

She could hear Josh in the shower. He was singing "Put Your Head on my Shoulder", by Paul Anka, and sounding just as good. She knew how much he loved old songs. He got that love from his grandmother.

Joey swayed along to the tune at the kitchen table whilst eating her food.

God, I love that man. How can I make it stop? Do I even want it to stop?

Josh entered the living room, with only a pink bath towel hanging from his toned waistline.

Joey swallowed the last piece of cereal in her bowl and rolled her eyes up to the ceiling.

Am I being punished for something that I don't know about?

She tried to ignore Josh, who was quietly singing the same song whilst rummaging around in a black holdall that was sitting on the sofa. She stood at the sink to wash up but found herself staring at the plughole, not wanting to run the tap and drown out his voice.

A smile grew on her face without her permission as Josh's arms snaked around her waist, gently rocking her from side to side to the song he was now singing close to her ear.

She tried to hide the bashful expression creeping onto her face as she allowed her body to be turned around by him and her hand to link into his. He loosened his grip and slowly spun her around and pulled her back towards him, resting her head down on his shoulder, and his head on the side of hers.

Joey closed her eyes, absorbing every movement, every touch, and every sound as they slow-danced in the kitchen to the song.

Josh gently let her go and smiled warmly into her eyes. 'I'd better get dressed.'

She watched him enter the bedroom, then she flopped to the floor and sprawled herself over the cream lino.

That's it. I'm going on strike. I simply refuse to move until someone explains to me why this is happening. It is completely unfair, in my opinion, not that it seems to count for anything. Nobody cares. Oh God, I'm a mess.

'Jo, what are you doing on the floor?'

She glanced up to see Josh standing over her with a look of confused amusement in those gorgeous blue eyes of his. At least he was now half dressed. Although, his toned torso and blue jeans look wasn't any easier for her than the pink towel look.

She sighed deeply. 'Oh, nothing.'

Nothing I can explain to you.

He lowered himself over her body, looking as though he were about to do a press-up.

She looked up at him. 'What are you doing?'

'Keeping you warm.'

'I am warm. You're the one half dressed.'

'You know, there's a bed in the other room, if you want to rest.'

'I don't want to go to bed.'

'You sure?'

Joey watched the creases appear around his mouth. She could see he was trying hard not to smile. 'I'm sure.'

You have no idea how much I want you right now, Josh Reynolds.

'Jo.'

'Hmm?'

'You've got bran flakes in your teeth.'

'Is it a good look?'

He grinned. 'Sexy as hell.'

She giggled and slapped the side of his arm. 'Get off me. I need to brush my teeth.'

He rolled onto his side and groaned as she headed for the bathroom.

I still haven't broken my resolution. I did not touch him. He touched me. He definitely touched me. Oh God, this is killing me.

19

Josh

Wishing Point was a large grassy area overlooking Pepper River. It was on slanted high ground, joining the quiet Pepper Bay to the livelier Sandly around the other side. It was known as a perfect picnic spot due to having the choice of the sea view from its clifftop end or the riverside at its bottom. Many dandelions often covered the area, and their seed heads gave the place its name. Wishes were made all the time by visitors blowing away the fluffy white balls into the wind.

Josh followed his brother up to the top end of Wishing Point. They had agreed to sprinkle their grandfather's ashes over the edge so that they floated off towards the sea, as was his dying wish.

Josh wasn't ready on the first day of the year. He wasn't ready to release his grandfather's ashes on any day of the year, but Jake had persuaded him that the 2nd of January was the time to say their final goodbye to the man who had raised them, because it wasn't fair to keep leaving it when it was what their grandfather had requested.

At the edge of the clifftop, Jake lowered himself to the ground so that he was lying flat on his stomach. Something he would do up there as a kid.

The ground was hard and dry, and the grass was dead and in need of healing from the snowstorm that had taken place a month before. There were no dandelions in sight, just the dark, cold sea below and a few seagulls above.

Josh joined his brother's side and peered over the edge at the long drop. 'Gran took Gramps up here for their first date. She said she brought her best blanket and was up at the crack of dawn baking fresh bread for the sandwiches she made. I guess she wanted it to be memorable.'

Jake laughed. 'It was memorable. Gramps got stung by a bee, and they had to go to the hospital because his hand started to swell up.'

'Gran said she knew she loved him the moment he came out of hospital and finished off the food in the hamper, all because she had made it for him.'

Jake glanced over his shoulder. 'Yeah, this place certainly was their favourite.'

'Gran told me Dad was conceived somewhere around here.'

Jake burst out laughing. 'Oh no. Too much information.'

Josh grinned widely. 'Gran was funny, wasn't she?'

They both looked down at the cold sea beneath them. The noise of the bitter wind whooshed past their ears, numbing the tips.

'We did this for Gran,' said Jake. 'Now we're doing it for Gramps.'

Josh looked at the tall pewter urn in Jake's hands. 'I can hear Gran telling us to get away from the edge.'

Jake laughed through his nose. 'Yep, and I can hear Gramps telling us to just get on with it.'

Josh touched his brother's arm. 'Wait. Let me check which way the wind is blowing. If that hits us in the face...'

'Gramps would crack up.'

'I won't be laughing.'

'You will.'

Josh stuck his index finger in his mouth, then held it in the air. He pointed left. 'That way.'

Jake's eyes were smiling at him. 'Yes, I gathered that by the direction my hair is blowing.'

Josh dangled one arm over the cliff. 'Hold it down low.'

Jake lowered both his arms over the edge, and Josh reached down and lifted the lid. The ashes of John Reynolds fell out.

They both looked left, watching the dusty particles disperse into the wind.

'Goodbye, Gramps,' whispered Jake. 'Thank you for everything you did for us.'

The lump that was stuck in Josh's throat forced him into silence. Instead of words, he saw pictures in the clear, cold sky. His grandfather was holding his grandmother's hand. They were smiling and waving. Their faces were filled with a lifetime of joy and laughter. Love radiated from them over towards their grandchildren. A figure of a slim man appeared by the side of his grandmother. He held a warm smile that widened when a woman stepped forward and took his hand. She blew a kiss towards Josh and Jake, and Josh almost reached out his hand to grab it, but his body was frozen to the dry grass beneath him. His eyes glossed over as he watched his parents fade into a passing cloud that had appeared from nowhere.

Jake's arm touched his shoulder, causing his head to jolt slightly and his eyes to blink. When he looked back for the cloud, it was gone, and so were his grandparents.

The wedged lump in his throat slipped down. 'They aren't here anymore, Jake.' He lowered his head so that it was resting on his arms. He kept his eyes open, in case they came back one last time. He wished so hard for them to return. Just one more moment. Just one last smile.

Jake's head gently rested upon his back.

Josh could feel his brother's body heat entering his spine, warming him. He felt soothed and loved, but it didn't stop his tears from falling.

Jake's arm reached over and tightly held him until his tears ran dry, his breathing settled, and he no longer needed holding.

* * *

Joey was sitting at the kitchen table in the flat, reading one of Josh's books, when he returned. Her gentle smile instantly removed his numbness.

'I made hot chocolate,' she said sweetly, nodding over towards the saucepan on the oven. 'I used soya milk and made sure the chocolate powder was vegan. I find myself checking everything now. It's still simmering. Do you want some?'

Josh removed his dark coat and kicked off his hiking boots. 'Thanks, Jo.'

She entered the kitchen to grab some mugs.

'How did it go?' she asked quietly.

He suddenly found himself standing behind her. His chest resting on her back. He couldn't remember moving away from the door.

She immediately turned and wrapped her arms around him, and he broke down in tears on her shoulder.

The loving touch of her hands circling his back and the soft whispers of reassurance close to her ear slowly eased his weary soul.

He took a calming breath as Joey reached behind her to grab a tissue from the box sitting on the side. He wiped his sore eyes and blew his nose and shoved the tissue into his cardigan pocket.

She placed her hands on his face, and he could see the concern in her eyes as she studied him for signs of what he was thinking. He knew his expression was blank because his mind was, but suddenly he had a need for her. His eyes darkened as his desire took over.

Joey gasped as he kissed her hard. He felt her fingers move into his hair, and he grabbed her tightly, lifting her body onto his. They stumbled back until the cupboard door held them in place. Her legs were wrapped around his waist, and her warm tongue was in his mouth. He pulled at her top as she pulled at his. Before he knew it, his grey cardigan and navy tee-shirt were on the kitchen floor. Her fingers were gripping his bare back, intensifying his need for her. He kissed down her neck, then found her opened mouth again. His heart was racing, and his love for her was overpowering his mind.

'No, stop,' she said, taking a breath.

Josh felt his head fall as she quickly moved her face away from his. He tried to control his heavy breathing. 'What's wrong?'

She wriggled her body until her legs were back on the floor. 'This isn't what you need right now.'

He leaned forward and tried to kiss her again. 'It is what I need.'

She turned her head away.

'I need you, Jo.'

'No, you don't. You need to rest today.' Her voice was soft but firm.

His brow creased as she walked away, leaving him standing in front of the cupboard door staring at his feet.

'Jo.'

He needed her to come back to him. He turned his head to see her wave him over to the sofa.

'Sit here,' she told him as he approached.

He didn't feel as though he were moving, but he was now sitting on the sofa, and Joey had put his tee-shirt back on him and had tucked a blue-and-yellow checked blanket over his lap.

'I'll get you that hot chocolate, and then we'll watch a film.'

20

Joey

The last couple of days had been nice and quiet for Joey to get on with some work, and she was pleased with the results of her dandelion lollipops so far. Josh had stayed at Starlight Cottage, so she had been sleeping at the flat on her own, and enjoying the peace.

She was so lost in her work, she jumped when she heard the shop door open. She went to call out from the back but stopped when she thought she heard someone crying. Slowly stepping away from the table, she peered outside at the shopfront.

Molly was slouched over one of the tables by the window, with her face buried in her arms. Her long dark hair was sprawled out over the top of her hands and pink gingham tablecloth.

Joey rushed over to her and sat by her side. 'Molly, what's wrong? What's happened?' She gently stroked her hair.

It was an effort for Molly to raise her head. Her bleary dark eyes peered over at Joey. 'I can't take it anymore, Jo.'

Joey placed her hand on Molly's arm. 'What can't you take anymore, Molls?'

Molly tried to steady her breathing through her sobs. 'I'm not allowed to talk about it.'

Joey frowned in annoyance. 'Says who?'

Molly sniffed and wiped her eyes with her fingers. 'My boyfriend.'

'I didn't know you had a boyfriend.'

'We've been together for two years now, Jo, but he doesn't want to let people know about us.'

Joey straightened her back. 'Why? Is he married?'

'No.'

'I'm lost, Molls. Why would he want to keep your relationship a secret for two years? Two years. That's a long time.'

Molly shrugged. 'I don't know, Jo. He's very private, but I think he just worries about commitment. All he sees is divorce and cheaters and thinks if he allows himself to go all in, it'll happen to him. Well, that's my theory.'

'Oh, Molly, you're too young to be dealing with all this heavy crap. You're twenty-five. You should be out there having the time of your life.'

Good grief, I'm starting to sound like Ruby.

'I love him, Jo, so much. I want to have the time of my life with him. Do you know how hard it is not being able to show the world how much you love someone? Not being able to kiss or hold them in public? Not spending important days together, like Christmas, for instance?'

I've got a pretty good idea. Yeah.

Joey brushed Molly's hair away from its stuck place on her damp cheeks. 'I know it's hard, Molls, but have you thought that maybe he's just not the one for you?'

'Why can't he just act like a normal person, Jo?'

Joey smiled warmly. 'Sounds as though he has issues. You need to talk them through with him.'

'I tried, just now, but he told me that I'm too young to understand. What kind of a statement is that?'

'Wait, how old is he?'

'Same age as you, but I don't care how old he is, it's still patronising.'

Joey nodded. 'I agree. You've been in this situation with him for two years. I'm pretty sure you understand him a lot better than he realises.'

'Give me some advice, Jo.'

You want me to help sort out your love life? If only you knew how crap I am at my own.

'I don't know what to say to you, Molly. I don't think there is anything either of us can do. This is up to him. He has to feel comfortable coming out in the open with you. He has to stop being afraid of love and start enjoying his relationship.'

'I just ended it with him.'

Joey leant forward and wiped away Molly's fallen tear and offered her a tissue from her pocket.

Molly sniffed and wiped her nose. 'I'm sorry to dump this on you, Jo, but I just feel so lost right now. I just ran in here. I only wanted him to tell me that he loved me, but he still couldn't say it. Two years later, and he still couldn't say those words to me. Have I done the right thing?'

'I don't know.'

The shop door flew open, causing Joey and Molly to jump.

Freddy was standing in the doorway. His face was flushed, his eyes were glossy, and his breathing was shaky. He stared straight over at Molly.

Joey looked straight at him. 'Fred, what's wrong with...' She stopped in her tracks as she witnessed the sorrow and pain glide between him and Molly. 'Wait, it's you. You're him. You're Molly's secret boyfriend.'

Freddy closed the door. 'I need to speak to you,' he said to Molly, whilst trying to avoid eye contact with Joey.

Joey stood up. 'You've got some nerve, Fred.'

Freddy's eyes rolled towards the floor.

Joey wasn't finished. 'It's not my place to interfere with your relationship, but you've been one of my best friends since we were born. You're like a cousin to me, so I'm bloody well going to tell you that the way you're treating Molly is beyond wrong. The girl loves you and has been with you for two years. If you don't love her, leave her alone. You've got no right messing with her heart like that.'

I need to reel myself in.

'Yeah, all right, Jo,' said Freddy, looking up. His expression looked like a cross between injured and aggravated. 'Can I just speak to Molly?'

Joey looked down at Molly.

Molly sniffed and nodded.

'I'll be just over here,' said Joey, heading for the counter.

Freddy sat in her chair.

Joey watched the two of them talking. She couldn't hear everything they were saying, as they kept their voices low.

Freddy and Molly have been together all this time and none of us knew. I guess you never really do know what's going on inside people's heads. We all thought they had a crush on each other, but that was it. Oh, look, he's holding her hand on the table. He looks genuinely concerned. She's smiling. At least she got rid of her snot bubbles before he came in. It wasn't the best look for her. Oh, he's touching her cheek now. This is so sweet. Please be making up. I can't believe I just got involved. Fred's going to hate me. He's kissing her. I think I'm going to melt. Oh my goodness. He's doing it publicly. Okay, so it's just me here, but still. This must be massive. He's made a breakthrough. He just said I love you. He did it. He said it. He told her. I want to do a happy dance. Oh, I love this. I want to hug them. I'd better not. Don't move. Don't breathe. Let them have their moment. Bloody hell, Molly's waited two years for this. It's a lot shorter than how long I've been waiting for Josh. Oh well, at least someone got their happy ending.

'You can come over now,' called out Freddy.

Joey innocently poked her head over the counter. 'Who me?'

He rolled his eyes at her. 'I know you were listening.'

She stepped forward. 'I wasn't.'

Freddy stood up. He held on to Molly's hand and smiled down at her. 'Joey Walker, allow me to introduce my girlfriend, my partner, Molly Hadley.'

Joey grinned widely as she closed in on them. She clutched her hands together in front of her heart. 'Oh, I'm so pleased for you both.'

Molly stood to snuggle under Freddy's arm, snivelling into his white shirt. Her face was filled with relief and joy.

Freddy gave Joey a hint of a smirk. 'Now, if you don't mind, Molly and I have some making up to do.'

Joey laughed through her nose. 'Now you're oversharing, Fred. Find the balance.'

Molly giggled as Freddy led her over to the door.

Joey heard Freddy tell Molly that he was going to take her up to Roseberry Cottage to see his mum.

Ruby will be so excited.

Joey looked out of the shop window at Pepper Lane as they left. She sighed deeply, feeling warm and cosy inside from the love she had just witnessed.

Oh, I feel as though I've just watched a really good Disney film. The princess finally got her prince, or in Molly's case, the chef.

Her eyes came back into focus as she stared at the bleak weather outside. Work was still being carried out at the riverbank, so she wasn't too worried about torrential rain any longer.

136

Nate caught her eye. He was walking up the slope, heading towards the pub.

Where did he just come from?

She opened the door and stepped outside to call over to him but stopped when she saw him wave up ahead. Turning her head, she could see Tessie waiting for him on the pub doorstep.

I wish those two would get together. Now that would be magical.

She looked back at her smiling brother just in time to see him lose his grin and suddenly freeze on the spot.

What's wrong with him?

Joey followed his eyes. She could see Freddy and Molly walking away in the distance, and then she saw something else.

Up at the end of the street, standing there with his hands in his pockets and facing uphill, was Josh, kissing Dana Blake.

All within a split second, Joey's mouth gaped, her heart stopped, and tears blurred her vision.

Dana pulled away from him and smirked, her pointy nose sneering down at Joey, and then she winked over at Nate.

Joey watched as Nate ran full speed ahead to grab Tessie before she reached Dana. He swung her petite body back inside the pub as she kicked and yelled in his arms.

Tessie's muffled voice wafted back into the street, 'I'm going to kill her.'

Dana gave a sharp flick of her long dark hair and grinned wickedly before walking away.

Josh, who hadn't moved from his spot the entire time, suddenly turned around.

Joey locked eyes with him and saw his expression change from blank to fearful.

'Joey, wait!' he cried.

There was no way in hell Joey was waiting to hear anything he had to say. She quickly turned on her heels and darted back inside the tea shop.

She was behind the counter when he burst in.

'Get out,' she yelled, throwing a chocolate muffin at him.

Josh flinched as the cake caught him on the side of his forehead. 'What the hell, Jo!'

'Get out,' she yelled again, throwing another muffin.

He batted it away. The crumbs splattered on the floor and the table that Freddy had just been sitting at with Molly.

Another muffin hit him on the shoulder.

'Jo, stop, please. I can explain.'

'I don't want to hear what you have to say. Get out.'

Another muffin hit his hair and crumbled on impact.

Josh pointed out his finger. 'You'd better stop throwing cakes at me, Jo.'

Joey's face was red, and her eyes teary. 'Why? What are you going to do about it?' She raised another muffin in the air.

Jake walked in just as Josh ducked. The muffin hit him on the shoulder. 'What the hell is going on here?' He glared down at the chocolatey mess surrounding his brother.

'Get him out,' she screamed.

Josh went to speak, but Jake manhandled him outside and closed the door on him, leaving him standing in the street flapping his arms up in the air.

'Joey, what has happened?'

Her shoulders slumped. She came out from behind the counter and practically fell down into a chair by the nearest table. She could barely believe what she had just witnessed, and now she had to say it out loud.

'He just kissed Dana Blake outside. I saw him. Nate and Tessie saw him. He didn't care who was watching. He just kissed her, Jake. How could he do that?'

Jake's face was filled with agitation. He glanced over his shoulder at his brother, who was still on the pavement. 'I'll deal with this.' He marched outside, slamming the door behind him.

Joey watched Josh get dragged away.

What the hell just happened? How has this happened? Why? Why?

She sniffed and rolled back the tears that were desperate to fall, feeling as though she'd been punched in the gut. There was no way to process the nightmare that had unfolded before her eyes.

Her mobile phone was vibrating over by the till. She got up to see that it was Wendall James calling her.

She sniffed again before answering. 'Hello, Wendall. Tell me you have some good news for me about Honeybee Cottage. I really need some good news right now.'

Joey's tired eyes widened. Her head straightened up, and the deep flush in her face returned.

'Say that again.'

She knew that Wendall had just told her that her dream cottage, the one she was supposed to get first refusal of, had been sold, but she also knew that her head was in a furious daze, so it was quite possible she had misheard.

She hadn't.

'I'm so sorry, Joey, but Honeybee Cottage has been sold,' said Wendall.

'But Loretta promised she would sell it to me. You promised I'd be the first to know, Wendall.' She paused as he tried to explain the situation, but she wasn't listening to him.

This isn't happening to me. It can't be.

'Wendall, stop talking,' she snapped.

'Listen, Jo…'

'No, you listen, Wendall. We had an agreement. I offered her the amount she asked for.'

'Someone offered her more.'

'What do you mean someone offered her more. Who, Wendall? Who offered her more?'

A short silence filled the air.

'Just tell me,' she yelled down the phone. 'Wendall, I swear to God, if you don't tell…'

'Josh Reynolds.'

'Say that again.'

Joey's mouth was left gaping as she slowly lowered the phone to the table as Wendall repeated himself. She stood and gazed lifelessly towards the front door for a second, and then something in her mind that looked a lot like rage jolted her back into the room. She ran for the door and flung it open.

I'm going to kill him.

Jake and Josh were arguing in front of The Book Gallery.

Joey's arm swept through the space between them, attempting to punch Josh straight on the jaw.

Josh stumbled back a step as Jake's quick reflexes caught her arm before it connected. 'Jesus Christ, Jo, what are you doing?'

Jake quickly grabbed her body. 'Jo, stop.'

Tears filled her eyes as she caught her shaky breath. 'Get off me, Jake. I'm going to kill him.'

Jake kept a firm hold of her wriggling body. 'No, Jo. You need to calm down.'

'Calm down? Calm down? He just bought Honeybee Cottage from under me.' She tried to kick him, but Jake spun her sideways. 'With all his millions, he had to go and do that. It's bad enough he's kissing that bitch in the middle of the street, but this. This!'

Josh was rubbing his jaw as though she had hit him there. He gave a half-shrug as he met his brother's furious eyes. 'What? I was going to tell you my news tonight.' He pulled a set of keys from his coat pocket. 'I just got the keys off Wendall. He dropped them off when he came here with Dana...' He stopped talking as though he knew he shouldn't have mentioned her name.

'Moving in with her, are you?' screamed Joey, desperately trying to get her hands on him.

Anna appeared in the shop doorway. 'Jake, let her go.'

'She's going to beat him up if I do.'

Anna looked Joey straight in the eyes. 'She won't. Let her go.' Her voice was low and composed.

Joey stopped struggling with Jake.

Jake released his hold, and Joey snatched the keys from Josh's hands and marched off up towards Honeybee Cottage.

21

Josh

Rain started to fall, dampening the brothers standing outside Anna's shop.

Jake was fuming. 'Josh, how could you do that?'

What am I missing here?

'Do what?'

'All of it,' snapped Jake. 'Dana bloody Blake, of all people, and in front of Nate. What the hell is wrong with you? You know what she did to him, and then you go and buy Honeybee. Could you be any more thoughtless, Josh? Totally unbelievable!'

'As I keep telling you, I did not kiss Dana Blake. She kissed me. I was standing there minding my own business when she suddenly appeared from nowhere and pushed her mouth onto mine.' He turned to Anna for some help.

He saw her eyebrows move upwards a touch.

'It's true,' he added. 'I was staring at the post box.' He pointed over to the small red letterbox built into the stone wall at the end of the road. 'I was visualising a painting. She just kissed me. I was in a zone. It wasn't until she pulled away and I saw her smirk over my shoulder that I realised what had happened.'

Jake stepped inside the doorway of the shop to shelter from the rain that was getting heavier. 'You had better sort this mess out, Josh.'

Josh wiped the water from his forehead. 'You were the one who wanted me to settle down somewhere, so I bought a cottage. Here, Jake, of all places, I bought one here, and now everyone's lost the plot.'

Anna peered around Jake's arm. 'Josh, Joey has been saving up to buy a cottage here for years. She was so excited when one became available, but mostly because Honeybee has always been her favourite. You just bought her dream home.'

'And you did it by outbidding her,' said Jake.

Oh, please, tell me you are winding me up.

He could tell by Jake's expression that Anna was telling the truth, the whole truth, and nothing but the truth.

'How much extra did you pay?' asked Jake.

Josh already knew that even if he said one penny, his brother's angry glare wouldn't soften. 'Fifty grand for her to sign on the dotted line straight away with no fuss.'

Anna's mouth gaped.

Disappointment washed across Jake's face. 'There's no way Joey would have been able to match or beat that.'

Josh flapped his arms to his sides. 'I didn't know she was buying it. Wendall never said. Loretta didn't tell me. I didn't know about this. I was just trying to secure the deal and get it wrapped up as quickly as possible. Loretta had already packed up and moved out days ago. Why didn't anyone tell me then? I didn't do this to hurt Joey. I did it to stick around. To show her I'm sticking around.'

'Perhaps you should tell her that,' said Anna, rolling her eyes in the direction of Honeybee Cottage.

'Perhaps you should tell her now before she destroys the place,' said Jake. 'She's got the keys, and she wasn't about to happily move in.'

Oh, shit!

Josh ran as fast as he could all the way up to Honeybee Cottage. The rain was belting down on him but didn't slow his movement. He just caught Joey slamming the door. He banged on the hard oak. 'Joey, open up.'

A small square side window opened. Joey's angry glare pierced through the misty raindrops. 'No.'

He watched the window slam shut. He banged on the door again. 'I'm getting soaked out here.'

Her voice yelled through the door. 'Good job. I hope you bloody drown.'

Thunder hit the sky, booming over Pepper Bay. The early-evening darkness crept in with the rumbling clouds.

Josh flicked his wet hair back. 'Joey, open this door right now, or I'll break it down.'

'Don't you dare,' said her muffled voice. 'It's a lovely door.'

He glared at it and then pushed his face closer to the framework. 'Joey, I'm sorry about Honeybee. I didn't know you were buying it. I promise you. I didn't know.'

Her voice sounded serious as she asked, 'Did you buy it for Dana Blake?'

Josh was starting to get sick to death of hearing that woman's name. 'Of course I didn't bloody well buy it for Dana Blake.' He thumped his fist on the wood.

'Why did you kiss her?'

'I didn't kiss her, Jo. She kissed me. She was the kisser, not me. I was the kissee. I swear to you, I did not kiss her back.'

He shivered as the dampness set in. His coat was warm but soaked, and his dark hair flopped lifelessly on his head. A small piece of chocolate muffin slid down his face, and he sighed deeply as he glanced around at the darkness. 'Joey, come on.'

She opened the window again. 'I hate you, Josh Reynolds, you cheating gazumping gazumper. This is my house.

You're not having it. You haven't changed. All you care about is yourself. Spiritual, my arse! Russell Brand wouldn't do this to me. You're nothing like him. You don't even have beads. Go away.' She slammed the window shut.

Russell Brand. What the hell!

'Jo, let me in.'

'Go and live with Dana Blake.'

He lowered his head and swore under his breath.

'Jo, I swear to God, if you don't open this door...' He stopped and took a calming breath, knowing he wouldn't get anywhere if he kept on shouting. He pressed his face against the wood and softened his voice. 'Jo, please let me in. I'm cold and wet, and it's dark out here now. You know I don't like the dark.'

He listened for a moment and then jumped back when the door clicked open. Slamming one hand on the wood, he pushed it wide, forcing her to stumble back. 'Ha! Fooled you.'

Joey's sorrowful face twisted back to hate. Before she had a chance to react, he picked her up and threw her over his shoulder and carried her outside into the heavy downpour.

'See how you like it.'

Joey kicked and screamed all the way to the gate at the front garden. 'Put me down.'

'Gladly.'

She gasped as he dropped her straight into a deep muddy puddle by the fence.

'Now, cool off,' he yelled.

He triumphantly marched back up the pathway towards the cottage and froze on the spot as a cold, wet clump of mud hit him straight on the back of his neck. He twitched as the soggy splodge slid down the gap between his collar and neck to meet his back. He tilted his head slightly and took a step forward. He stilled as another gooey lump of mud hit him in the exact same spot. He took a steady breath and turned to see Joey sitting in the puddle right where he left her.

She was holding up a blob of dripping mud that was sliding through her clenched fingers and running down her arm.

'Throw it at me,' he said through gritted teeth. 'I dare you.'

Their defiant eyes remained locked in a standoff. Neither of them moving as the heavy rain continued to beat down on their stiff bodies.

Josh made a grunting sound, gave a slight smirk, and turned back to the cottage. Mud flew past the side of his face, slapping his ear.

'Right!' he snapped, turning sharply to her.

Joey let out a gasp and attempted to scramble away, but she wasn't fast enough.

He grabbed her and pulled her back down again.

She landed on all fours, and he flipped her over and pinned her down in the muddy puddle. She struggled with him, trying to free herself, but he was stronger.

He reached down and grabbed a handful of slosh and smeared it in her hair. 'How do you like those apples?'

Tears filled her eyes as her body weakened beneath him. She softly gazed up into his bright glare. 'Josh.' Her voice was a broken whisper.

He stilled, gazing back at her. Wanting her. Needing her.

'You're hurting me,' she added, just as quietly.

Oh, crap!

He quickly removed himself from her body. 'I'm so sorry, Jo. Are you all right?'

She stood and waited for him to find his feet, and as he was doing so, she quickly shoved him with all of her might.

Josh fell down onto his bottom straight into the puddle.

'Ha! Fooled you,' she yelled. 'Check bloody mate.'

Josh's mouth flapped open and closed like a fish.

She made a quick dash for the door, but his foot stopped her from slamming it.

They struggled with the hefty lump of oak between them, but he won the battle.

She ran into the empty living room and stopped in front of the dead fireplace.

He slammed the door and stood in the hallway, staring over at her.

She turned her back on him and slumped down to the silver-grey carpet. She sat cross-legged, staring at the cold ashes in the grate.

He calmly walked over to her and sat by her side.

They watched the non-existent fire in silence as wet mud slid down their faces.

Josh spoke first. 'I'm sorry, Jo.'

She lowered her head.

22

Joey

Joey felt deflated in every sense. She also felt cold, wet, and in need of a hot shower. She shook her head, purposely flicking mud from the scraggly ends over onto Josh.

She held back her grin as his eye flinched, and then she took a slow, deep breath. 'I'm tired, Josh.'

'Yeah, I know.'

There was something about his gentle tone that soothed her. She gazed out at the dark room and shivered.

Josh removed his soaked coat and draped it over her shoulders. 'For what good it'll do.'

The coat felt heavy and only pushed her wet clothes further into her body.

What has happened to us? How did we end up like this? What a mess. It's gone so wrong.

'Do you hate me, Josh?'

She could see the lines on his brow appear from her peripheral vision, they went that deep.

'Of course I don't hate you.'

Silence loomed for a few seconds.

'I just gave you my coat.'

A slow smile built on her face, against her will, but she wasn't happy.

I feel too numb to cry. I really need to cry. Cry. Sleep. Wake up. New day. Cry all over again. I've got nothing left inside me.

Josh's chest rose and fell. 'I didn't kiss her, Jo. I was just standing there looking at the post box. She stepped in front of me and... well, you know the rest.'

I don't know what to say to you, Josh. I can't even think straight right now.

Josh exhaled deeply again. 'I didn't even take my hands out of my pockets.' He sounded as though he were talking to himself. He shifted his weight so that he was facing her. 'Jo, I didn't know about this place. I swear to you. I would never do that to you. I would never hurt you. Never.'

You do nothing but hurt me. It hurts when you're near me. It hurts when you leave me. It hurts when I think about you. It hurts when I look at you. I can't do this anymore. I seriously can't cope with any more pain. Dana was on his mouth. I feel sick. He said he didn't kiss her back. I have to believe that. He wouldn't do that to me. He said he didn't. He didn't.

She quickly swiped the tear away that had escaped the corner of her left eye.

'Okay,' she mumbled.

Josh frowned. 'Okay what?'

'I believe you.'

'About both things?'

She gave a half-nod and watched relief fill his bright eyes.

'I know how much she hurt your brother, Jo. I wouldn't touch her with a barge pole. I feel sick thinking about it.'

We both need to stop thinking about it. I can't have that in my head any longer.

'Then stop thinking about it.'

'Can we talk about this place now?'

'What is there to say?'

'It's yours, Jo. You can have the cottage.'

What? Is he serious?

She turned to face him. He looked serious. He looked like Jake.

Josh pulled in his lips and nodded.

'But you want to live here, Josh.'

He shrugged, looking worn out. 'I don't want it now. I'm not taking away your dream home. I'll sign it over to you tomorrow.'

'I can't let you do that.'

'Yes, you can. It should be yours. You worked so hard for it.'

'It feels different now.'

'I know. I'm sorry. I've ruined it for you.'

She wiped some mud from her cheek that had dripped down from her hair, then looked glumly at her hand.

If I take him up on his offer, he'll have nowhere to go. He won't stay at his gran's forever. He will leave Pepper Bay. Probably for good. I don't want to lose him again. I can't handle this.

'Where would you live?'

'I'll stay at Gran's till something else comes up. There are properties in Sandly for sale. I liked this place because it has a cabin out the back. I was going to use it as my art studio.'

Joey's eyes widened. 'So, you won't leave the island?'

His eyes glossed over as they almost twinkled at her. 'I'm not leaving here, Jo. I'm going to make this place headquarters from now on.'

She felt her heart warm and her head whirl. A sudden thought sprung to mind, so she blurted it out before she had time to dissect the idea. 'We could share the cottage.'

Josh looked amused. 'Share? What do you mean? You'd have it four days a week, and I'd have the rest?'

She breathed out a short, sharp laugh. 'No. I mean we could live here together. That is, until another cottage becomes available, then one of us could take that. You can still use the cabin for your artwork. I'm out most of the time at work anyway, so we wouldn't get under each other's feet or anything. I don't know. It's just a suggestion.'

'It sounds perfect. I'll still sign it over to you, and I'll sort of be like your lodger. I'll even pay you rent.'

'You'd have to. I can't afford the mortgage now that you've upped the price tag.'

Josh smiled. 'Jo, you don't have a mortgage. I don't have a mortgage. It's yours. I'm giving it to you.'

Joey recoiled. 'I don't feel comfortable about that. I have the deposit. I could give you that, and then pay the rest in instalments to you over the course of... well, my entire life, I guess.'

'Or you could use the money you have saved to fix this place up. I know you'll want your own style in the kitchen.'

'Josh...'

'How about we go back to the flat, pick up the mattress from the spare room, bring it over here and sleep right in front of the fire tonight.'

Joey felt her stomach churn from the hundred butterflies that had just taken flight.

He gently touched her knee. 'I haven't had time to get the electricity switched on yet, but look, there's half a log sitting beside the fireplace. We can burn that. I'll switch the water on so we can still brush our teeth and have a wash. We'll bring back a few supplies. You can get a feel for the place and make your decision in the morning.'

'The mattress will get soaked on our way over.'

'Nah, we'll wrap it in bin bags and tape. Besides, listen. It sounds as though it's died down out there. Come on, Jo. We can do this. We've slept in a barn together, a car, out in the open up at Wishing Point. I'm sure we can do this.'

151

'We can have a hot shower first and come over in our PJs and wellies. I can make some sandwiches and bring some drinks and cake.'

Josh grinned. 'As long as it's not chocolate muffins.'

23

Josh

The heat from the shower was welcomed wholeheartedly, as Joey pointed out to a chilly, half-naked Josh standing in the bathroom on the other side of the curtain, waiting his turn.

'Oh, gross,' she muttered.

'What is it?'

'I've got lumps of mud entangled in my hair.'

Josh laughed to himself. 'Sorry, Jo. Do you want me to help you wash it out?'

'If you wouldn't mind.'

I wasn't expecting that.

He quickly removed his tee-shirt and climbed into the bath to stand behind her, scanning her naked body that he knew so well. He wanted to place his hands on the curve of her hips. He watched her glance over her shoulder. Her taupe eyes rolled straight down to his black boxer shorts.

'You know I'm naked, right?'

'I wasn't totally sure you would be.'

She frowned. 'Why wouldn't I be?'

'Because I was on the other side of the curtain. I wasn't sure if that would make you keep your underwear on.'

Joey turned back to look up at the showerhead. 'You've seen my body more times than I can count. We've had numerous showers together. Besides, I'm not showering in my underwear.'

Josh looked down at his boxers. 'Do you want me to remove mine?'

'I think you should keep yours on.'

Yeah, I think that would be the safest bet.

She lowered her head. 'Pass me a towel. I'll wrap that around me. We made rules, and I just forgot myself for a moment.'

It's a bit late for a towel.

He stretched outside the bath and grabbed a large pink towel and handed it to her.

She wrapped it around her body, tucking it beneath her arms.

He moved closer to her back and placed his hand around her arm. 'Give me some shampoo.'

She reached out to the rusty metal stand screwed into the corner of the wall that stretched from the bath to the ceiling. A bottle of Jake's almond milk shampoo was sitting on one of the four shelves.

'I see you've pinched Jake's shampoo,' she said, laughing slightly. 'I was using my own until I saw this sitting in here. It's so lovely.'

'I thought he wouldn't notice. He had five bottles. He noticed.'

Joey giggled.

He looked down at the creamy liquid she had squirted in his hand and gently wiped it down her hair. He stared, almost mesmerised, as he tentatively massaged her head. He flicked a lump of sticky mud down into the bath and grinned to himself.

'Argh!' he cried.

He watched her body stiffen with fright. 'What?'

'It's a worm.'

Joey gasped and slapped her hands over her eyes. 'Oh my God, Josh. Get it off me.'

'I'm not touching it.'

Her hand fell backwards to slap his arm. 'Get it off me, Josh. Get it off.'

He couldn't hold back his laugh any longer. 'I was just kidding.'

He heard her swear under her breath. She turned to him, with one soapy eye shut. 'Are you sure there aren't any worms in my hair?'

'Calm down, Medusa. You're good.'

'I'd turn you to stone,' she huffed out.

He wiped the shampoo from her eye. 'Oh, you'd like me rock hard.'

Joey laughed out loud. 'Oh yeah? You reckon it still works after such a long timeout?'

Josh frowned down at his boxers. 'Yeah, it still works. Turn around. Let me finish your hair.'

Before my celibacy goes out the window.

She did as she was told, and he carried on with the task at hand whilst still grinning to himself.

Five more strokes of her shoulder-length locks and Josh had lost his sense of humour. He slowly guided her around to face him and tilted her head back slightly so that he could rinse away the foam. He concentrated on what he was doing so that he didn't get shampoo in those brown-grey eyes that were watching his every move.

The noise of the falling water was the only thing disturbing the intense atmosphere between them.

He tried hard to avoid her eyes. His breathing was speeding up, and he was doing everything he could to slow it back down.

Her hand touched his chest, and he was sure his heart had skipped a beat, because he had a sudden lightheaded feeling that lasted only a second.

His hands slid slowly down her arms to stop at her wrists, where his thumb stroked the back of her right hand. 'Turn around.'

She did and her towel fell down. She quickly bent to retrieve it. 'I'm sorry. I wasn't trying to do the sexy towel slip manoeuvre. It just got really heavy.'

He took the towel from her and threw it to the back of the bath. 'Let's just lose the towel.' He stared at the shape of her back for a moment.

You're so beautiful.

He gravitated forward and rested his mouth close to her shoulder.

'What do you want?' she asked.

The tone of her voice told him she wasn't talking about shower products.

Every. Single. Part. Of. You.

Josh swallowed hard. He felt his brow tighten. He couldn't do this again with her. Sex wasn't what he wanted from her. He wanted her to love him. Make love to him. With him.

Jo, you're killing me. I can't breathe.

He took a step back. 'Give me some more shampoo. I'll give it a second wash.'

He waited.

She didn't move.

'Jo.'

She poured some more creamy liquid into his hand.

As soon as he started to wash her hair, she placed her hands on her head to join in with his movements.

Together, they slowly caressed each other's fingers. The sensual motion caused him to call upon every technique he had been taught about the art of self-control.

What can I see? What can I smell? What can I taste? I can see her. I can smell her. I can taste her. Oh God, this isn't working. Coal. Think about coal. I wonder what it tastes like. Probably chalky. I really don't care about coal right now. Look at her. I know what you want, Jo, but I can't. I won't do it. I'll only feel like crap afterwards for giving in. It can't be this way between us anymore. Just fall in love with me and everything will change for us. I'll give you what you want and more. I'm staying now. I'm not your holiday fling. I'm going to be here for you. Just bloody well notice me as something more than your sex toy or I'll have to think about coal for the rest of my life.

Joey turned around to rinse her hair. She closed her eyes as the water poured over her face.

Josh took a breath whilst she wasn't watching him. He lowered his arms and stepped back. He was just about to escape when she looked at him. He felt his heart jolt from the request in her eyes.

'Do you want me to help you now?' she asked, stepping closer.

'No. I'll only be five minutes.'

She got the message.

He closed his eyes as her body brushed past him to exit the bath from the other end. He exhaled as quietly as possible and stepped under the showerhead. He quickly washed his hair, then switched the temperature down to cold.

24

Joey

The rain had died down outside, but Joey and Josh still used numerous black bin bags and parcel tape to cover the mattress they had dragged out from the spare room.

'I've got two pillows in one carrier bag,' said Joey, 'and a couple of hand towels in another. I also have toothbrushes, toothpaste, water, and a hairbrush. Oh, and I got a bag of food. Not sure how we're going to carry all this though.'

'Bags on our arms and mattress over our heads. Should be okay. Put your dressing gown and wellies on. Put our slippers in a bag. Oh, we need a lighter.'

Joey grabbed a box of matches from the kitchen draw and tossed it into one of the white cloth bags. 'Okay. Let me take the bags down first.'

On her way back up to the flat, she met the mattress coming down the stairs.

'This is awkward,' came Josh's voice from the top end. 'Mind it doesn't fall on you, Jo.'

She giggled and grabbed at its side, tugging it towards her.

The hefty mattress slid down the steps and bumped her chest, causing her to slip back.

'You okay down there?' asked Josh, peering over the top.

Joey struggled to manoeuvre the bed out of the doorway. 'I'm… I… Yeah, I'm okay. It's a bit tricky.'

The mattress was jammed on a bend. Josh gave it one hard shove, and it practically hurled itself at Joey.

She let out a faint scream as she found herself trapped between the bed and shop counter.

Josh came around to her side. 'Hmm, vulnerable. I think I might leave you like this.'

'Get it off me.'

He moved the mattress away so that she was free and slid it over to the front door. 'Right, let's get you loaded up first.' He placed a bag on each of her arms and then put the rest on his.

'You'll have to hold the bed while I lock the door behind us,' she said, stepping outside into the light rain.

Josh struggled to lift the bed on his own. It was a double and hard to grip, but he managed to lift it above his head.

She giggled and quickly got underneath. 'Well, at least I'm dry now.'

'Bloody well hold it with me, Jo.'

Silently laughing behind his back, she reached up her hands and helped lessen the burden.

They started walking up Pepper Lane.

She lowered her arms for a second. 'Oh goodness, this isn't as easy as I thought it would be.'

'Jo, have you let go?'

'No,' she lied, putting her hands back up.

'Not far to go.'

Joey scrunched her nose up at his attempt to motivate her.

'Good thing it's close by,' he added.

Her shoulders were aching, so she lowered her arms again. 'Yeah, we're doing really well.'

'You've let go, haven't you?'

She glanced down at the bags she was holding. 'I'm helping, Josh.' She grinned to herself, then leant forward and tickled his ribs.

159

His body squirmed away from her fingers. 'Get off me, Jo.'

'Who's vulnerable now?' She tickled him again.

'Jo, I swear to God, I'll drop this on your head.'

She giggled and raised her hands to help carry the bed.

They continued to struggle all the way into Honeybee Cottage.

Joey was relieved to place the bed on the carpet in front of the fireplace, even though Josh had done most of the heavy lifting. She quickly unwrapped the mattress so they had something to sit on.

The room was dark and the house quiet.

'I brought a candle for the bathroom.' She waved it in the air as she watched Josh light the fire.

He sat next to her. 'That's better.'

She warmed under him as he put his arm around her and rubbed down her arm.

'You cold, Jo?'

'I'm okay.'

He nodded at the bags on the floor. 'What did you bring for dinner?'

She turned to the nearest bag and rummaged inside. 'Well, there wasn't much at the flat.' She pulled out an avocado.

He raised his eyebrows in amusement. 'That's my dinner?'

'Wait.' She revealed a packet of rice cakes.

'Did you bring a knife?'

'Oh, I forgot about cutlery.'

'What have you got?'

She wiggled a small foil-wrapped package. 'Salad cream sandwich.'

'Healthy.'

'I did bring a fruitcake. I made it yesterday. It's completely vegan.'

A wide smile built on his face. 'Did you make that for me?'

'Yes. You're lucky I didn't throw that at you.'

He waved his fingers at her. 'Give me that and a bottle of water.'

She handed him the food and drink and studied his face as he took a bite of her untested vegan cake. 'Is it moist? I used coconut oil. Can you taste the pumpkin spice? I didn't use much.'

He seemed to be enjoying it. His head was nodding and he was smiling.

'Try it yourself,' he said, offering her a piece of his handful.

She allowed him to place the sample inside her mouth. Her lips brushed against his fingers, but she was concentrating too much on the flavour of her cake to think about him feeding her.

Sunflower oil next time. More spice. Less cranberries. Not bad.

'Do you like it?' she asked. 'It needs tweaking.'

'I love it. Thanks for making me a cake.'

She got up and put her slippers on.

'Where are you going?' he asked, opening his water bottle to take a sip.

She lit the candle and dripped some of its wax onto a saucer. She stuck the candle in place and headed towards the hallway. 'I'm going to look around.'

He laughed. 'In the dark?'

She shrugged. 'Why not?'

She walked into the large empty kitchen. Even in the glimmer of candlelight she could see that the cupboards were

161

white and shiny. The two windows in the room were bare and the back door matched the front one. She knew exactly what she wanted to do with the place.

Upstairs was cold, and three out of the four bedrooms gave the impression that they had never been used. Their walls were plain and the flooring was polished pine planks. The main bedroom had flowery wallpaper and a soft cream carpet. Pastel-green curtains and a brushed-cotton lampshade had been left behind.

Joey went over to look outside the window at the back garden.

She couldn't see any signs of life anywhere. She smiled to herself as thoughts of her bedroom view at Pepper Pot Farm came to mind. She loved looking uphill at Starlight Cottage. Even when Josh wasn't there, she would imagine he was. She would sometimes visualise him standing at his bedroom window with his binoculars waving down at her while she did the same to him. There were nights when she lit the candle on her windowsill in hope that wherever he was in the world he would sense her presence in his life and miss her so much he would come home.

The candle in her hand flickered, bringing her out of her thoughts.

The outbuilding was visible. It would be filled with Josh's art equipment soon and that made her happy. Now she would be able to watch him from the window while he did the one thing in the world that he loved the most.

This house really could be mine. He said so. He meant it. This could be my bedroom. I'll need lights for the garden. I need to see something outside in the night. I won't be able to see Josh's bedroom anymore. I'll see a wall. He'll be on the other side of the wall. Not sure I like that idea. Would I feel lonely here? Would I miss my family? There is plenty of room. Gran can stay over whenever she wants, and Daisy.

She wiped away a falling tear.

I miss home already. What if I can't move? What if I end up alone here? I'll be like Ruby Morland. She does all right living up in Roseberry Cottage by herself. I'll be fine. Josh said he's not leaving anyway. But what if he does? What if he doesn't? How am I going to cope with him here with me but not with me? Can I deal with that? What kind of messed up relationship have I got with this man? Is this making things worse? Am I making my life harder? I wish someone would tell me what to do.

'See anything out there, Jo?'

She gazed out into the night. Her shoulders felt lead-heavy and her head a little giddy from overthinking. 'Not much.'

The warmth from his body heat reached beneath her cream dressing gown as he leaned over her shoulder.

'Just the cabin for your studio,' she added.

She could sense that he was smiling.

'Looks perfect,' he whispered.

25

Josh

'You know, if you make this your bedroom, I can wave up to you when I'm working down there.'

Joey's head rested softly under his arm. He lowered his gaze to look at the top of her head, wanting to kiss her hair, hold her tighter, make love to her on the soft cream carpet beneath their feet.

I miss you, Jo. I miss you when I'm gone, and I miss you when I'm here.

'We could add some lights to the garden,' he said quietly.

'I was just thinking that.'

His mouth smiled but nothing else.

I used to put a candle in my window whenever I was away and needing you. I wish I could tell you that. If I knew for sure it wouldn't damage what we do have, I would tell you the truth. Why can't you be like those women who want marriage, commitment? Why do you only want a summer love and a quick fumble in the hay? Are you afraid of love? I guess it's not your fault. Everyone sees me as a playboy.

Joey shivered and placed her arm around his waist.

He tightened his hold on her. 'Come on. Let's get in bed. It'll be warmer.' He led her back downstairs to the living room.

The log in the fire was burning nicely, giving the room a warm golden glow. Bin bags were ripped and scrunched up over in the corner and cloth carrier bags had been moved away from the made bed.

Joey blew out the candle and placed it on the stone fireplace, beside the grate. She climbed on the mattress and rolled on her side, away from the heat.

Josh settled down between her and the fire. He turned his head to face her back.

She's gone quiet. Probably thinking about this place. What a day. I wasn't expecting any of this when I woke up this morning. I'm going to have words with Wendall when I see him. What a bloody nightmare. I can't believe he didn't say anything.

'I'm sorry I nearly punched you in the face,' came her muffled voice.

Oh, so that's what you're thinking about.

'That's okay.'

She shifted her body so that she was on her side, facing him. 'It's not okay, Josh. I've never hit anyone in my life. I'm not violent.'

'If someone did to me what you thought I had done to you, then I'd probably want to smack them one as well.'

Her hand reached out to gently trace over his jawline. Her eyes were on his mouth, and her voice was low and husky. 'I'm so glad I didn't hurt you.'

He held her hand to stop it from moving across his face.

You only hurt my heart, Jo.

'It's fine. I'm fine.'

He noticed a glossy look appear in her eyes. He knew it wasn't from tiredness or the reflection of the fire.

'Come here, Jo.'

He pulled her closer to his body, and she snuggled into his chest. He held her hand up by his mouth and kissed her knuckles. 'We'll have to get you some boxing lessons.'

He heard a muffled laugh. 'Stop it.'

The crackling noise in the grate filled the room.

165

Josh closed his eyes and secretly inhaled her lemon scent. A shadow of dull disappointment covered his heart. He wanted to feel more than just content. He wanted the whole package. Happiness, peace, and love. He wanted Honeybee Cottage to be their home. Joey to be his wife. To have a family with her. A life. He took a deep breath and felt her adjust herself on his chest.

Joey Walker, if you only had half a clue what I feel around you, perhaps you would see me differently. I'm not helping by lying here with you. None of this was supposed to happen. I had a plan. I wasn't going to be so wrapped up in you this time. I was going to take things slowly. Really slowly. Maybe I should just tell her. Get it out there. Maybe now's good. Maybe now's not so good. I don't want her to leave. She might if I go all serious on her. Actions speak louder than words. I've just got to be patient. She'll see my actions. She'll see me not leaving. She's going to take me seriously. She has to.

Joey tapped his tee-shirt. 'Do you want to come to the January Fair with me tomorrow? It'll be something fun to do after this crappy day.'

A day out together would be perfect.

'Sounds great.'

He felt her body soften. He was pleased she was so relaxed in his arms.

'Today hasn't been all bad,' he added.

'No, it hasn't. I got to witness love today. Freddy finally came out of the closet about his relationship with Molly. It was so adorable to watch. I'm so glad they're together. I'm happy that he's letting the world know that she's his girlfriend. What was the good part for you today?'

Josh smiled smugly to himself. 'You kept the eternity ring on even when you hated my guts.'

166

'I love my ring.'

I love you. Change the subject.

'So, Freddy and Molly, eh?'

'Hmm. It was like watching the end of a romance film, when the couple finally get together.'

I hope we have that. I can't talk about love right now. Not while we're like this. Think of something else before your heart takes over, Reynolds. If I don't control this, I'll be making love to her in about five minutes. I could do that right now. I could just move my body, lift her onto me, reach for her face... Argh! No. Shut up. Focus. What were we talking about? Ah, yes.

'I've never been to the January Fair before.'

'You don't come here for Christmas often, Josh, and when you do, you've normally left by now.'

He exhaled and was pleased it didn't come out shaky. 'I'll probably still travel from time to time, but I'm staying here now.'

'I'd like to travel.'

'Yeah? Where would you like to go?'

'Malta.'

'Oh, I wasn't expecting you to say that. Do you know, I haven't actually been there myself. Why Malta?'

Joey started to twiddle with his top. 'My mum and Ruby went there on holiday when they were young. Ruby told me all about it. They went on a daytrip out on a boat that took them to a place called the Blue Grotto. They went in and out of caves, where the air turned cool and the sea was turquoise. She said the boat was low in the water, and they kept thinking that the sea would come in the boat, and Mum was scared, but even though she felt that way, she loved being in the caves, because the rocks felt like magical homes where no one would ever find her. I'd like to see those caves.'

He placed his hand over hers. 'It sounds lovely, Jo. We can be sleeping in Malta tomorrow night, if you want.'

She twisted her head towards his face. 'Really?'

'Sure. We can fly there in the morning. I'll just need to make a couple of calls and we'll be sorted.'

She grinned widely, revealing her perfect teeth. 'Is that what it's like being rich, you just fly off somewhere whenever you feel like it?'

He looked deeply into her enquiring eyes. 'I guess so. Never really thought about it before.' He watched her lower her head.

There was a moment of silence.

'I don't want to go tomorrow,' she said quietly.

He stroked her back. 'I'll take you there whenever you're ready.'

'Maybe in the summer. I'll have saved some more money by then, especially when I start selling my lollipops. They're going to be world famous, you know. Meanwhile, we have a funfair to attend.'

Josh smiled and kissed her head.

26

Joey

During January every year, Hope Park in Sandly hosted a funfair for the whole month. It was designed to help bring light and cheer to a dreary month and offer a happy, fun start to the new year. It was filled with stalls that had stripy roofs, arcade games, noisy bumper cars and spinning Waltzer rides, a green-and-white helter-skelter and a big red Ferris wheel. There was a large grey food tent, and lots of sweets and popcorn machines dotted around. Multicoloured lightbulbs draped everywhere, and wooden, some parts uneven, boards made the floor. Lively fairground music filled the hotdog-infused air, encouraging all guests to join in with the excitement.

Joey happily entered the park with Josh. Jake and Anna were holding gloved hands in front of them, and Nate and Tessie were being dragged over to the bumper cars by their daughters as soon as they stepped foot inside the funfair.

A woman in a red coat approached Josh. 'Hey, I thought it was you.'

Josh smiled warmly. 'Oh, hello again.' He turned to Joey. 'This is Dolly. She's taking over her aunt's shop, Dolly's Haberdashery.'

Dolly tucked a loose strand of her mousey hair back under her multicoloured woolly hat. 'Hello.'

Josh nodded towards Joey. 'This is Joey. The one I told you about.'

Dolly held a bubbly smile. 'Ah, yes, Edith's Tearoom, right?'

'That's right,' said Joey. 'Sorry to hear about your aunt shutting up shop. She's been there since I was a kid. She told me her niece would be taking over.'

'I think she wanted to retire anyway,' said Dolly. 'The shop was starting to wear her out.'

'Will you keep it the same?' asked Joey.

'I plan to keep some stock. I have my own online business. I make scented candles. I was going to sell off all the old stock in the shop, but then Josh came in when I was there and bought a photo frame, and it made me think twice about selling certain things, so I'll keep some of the stuff that can be sold as gifts and make it more of a gift shop. Well, that's my plan at the moment. I want to keep the shop sign as well, but it'll just be the Dolly part. I haven't thought what to add to it yet. Mind you, I wasn't expecting to own a shop, but when my aunt came up with the idea, I thought, why not. I'm forty now, so why not try something new. Well, that was my motivation anyway.'

Joey smiled. 'Well, you feel free to pop over to the tea shop anytime. The first slice of cake is on me, as a welcome to Pepper Bay.'

Dolly snuggled her rosy cheeks lower into her multicoloured scarf. 'Thank you so much. I'm going to move into the flat above the shop as well, so I'll be popping in for a coffee quite often, I reckon.'

'When are you moving in?' asked Josh.

'I'm hoping I'll have everything sorted by early spring.'

'Well, we look forward to having you join Pepper Lane, Dolly,' said Joey, giving her a gentle pat on the arm.

Dolly's big chestnut eyes gleamed. 'Oh, thank you. I was a bit worried about moving somewhere new.'

'As soon as you move in, I'll take you over the pub to meet everyone,' said Joey. 'You'll soon feel right at home.'

'Thank you. I don't feel so nervous now.' Dolly glanced over her shoulder. 'Anyway, I better get off. My aunt's waving at me. She wanted me to bring her here today, but I think it's actually for my benefit. As you can tell by my accent, I'm from Ireland, but I've been living in Hastings for a good few years, and now she wants me to fall in love with everything the Isle of Wight has to offer. I will admit, it is a beautiful place. Anyway, I'll see you both again soon.'

'See you soon, Dolly,' said Josh.

Joey gave a slight wave as Dolly smiled. 'It was nice to meet you.' She turned to Josh and linked her arm with his.

Josh tightened his grip on her, pulling her closer to his body. 'You know, I'd forgotten what a friendly bunch you Pepper Bay lot are.'

She rolled her eyes up at him in amusement. 'Yes, we welcome all sorts.'

He laughed through his nose and looked around at the fair. 'So, what do you want to do first?'

She quickly headed for the helter-skelter. 'The slide. I have got to see you on that.'

He laughed. 'What have I let myself in for?'

Tessie was at the bottom by the time Josh came hurtling down the slide with Joey in between his legs. She quickly snapped a picture of them and smiled at their laughter.

'The girls are on the bumper cars,' she said, 'and Nate's struggling to fit inside one. It's so funny. You have to come and look.'

Joey raised her eyebrows in amusement at her large, muscular brother, who was trying to squeeze into a small bumper car.

'I fit,' he yelled over to them, then drove off to catch up with Robyn and Daisy.

Joey shook her head. 'What does he look like?'

'Come on, Jake,' urged Anna, tugging his arm towards the cars.

Jake's face was such a picture, Tessie made sure she caught the expression on her camera.

'Please,' added Anna.

Much to everyone's surprise, Jake climbed in a car. Anna beamed with delight, and Jake frowned as Nate immediately bashed into him and laughed loudly.

'Get him, Jake,' yelled Joey.

'Come on,' said Tessie, putting her phone in her bag. 'Let's all go.'

Josh paid the waiting ticket boy, as everyone had seemed to forget about that part, and then joined in with the chaos.

Tessie tried to stop to take photos but nearly dropped her phone as Joey and Anna cornered her.

Jake was bumping everyone who dared near him or Anna, and Josh kept away from Joey's car at all times, which did make her wonder why.

After no injuries and a lot of laughter, their cars stopped and they were waved off the track.

Jake seemed more upset than anyone else to leave the cars behind until Anna told him he could have another go later on.

Joey watched her brother win more cuddly toys than anyone else and felt slightly left out when he handed a large giraffe to Tessie and an armful of smaller animals to Daisy and Robyn. She tried desperately to place a basketball through a hoop numerous times to win the giant panda she had her eye on but just couldn't manage it. Even Anna was holding a meerkat that Jake had won for her.

Josh appeared at her side. 'Which one do you want?'

'You can't just buy it.'

She saw amusement sweep through his eyes as he handed over some money to the young girl behind the stall and lifted a ball.

'How many do I need to get?' he asked the girl.

'Three,' she replied, looking bashful as he curled his mouth her way.

Joey rolled her eyes. 'Go on then, hotshot. Let's see what you've got.'

Three hoops later and Joey was embracing a rather large cuddly panda bear, and Josh hadn't said a word about it. He just offered a smug smile and a cheeky wink.

The Ferris wheel was something that Joey had always avoided. The one at the January Fair wasn't too big, but it still made her wary. She wasn't scared of heights, but she wasn't overly keen on them either. This year, she wanted to step outside her comfort zone and challenge herself. Having Josh by her side made the daunting ride seem bearable.

She sat in the swaying seat with him, with the panda squashed in between them.

Josh frowned down at the toy and lifted it out from under the metal bar. He tossed it over at his brother. 'Jake, catch.'

Joey watched her panda fly through the air and then Josh's body slide closer to hers. The wheel turned, and so did her stomach.

I can do this. It's just a ride. It'll be over in a minute. Just focus on the scenery.

The wobbly seat did little to ease her nerves.

I want to get off. I'm trapped. I don't like it. Why did I do this?

The acid in her gut churned and heat rushed to her face. Her heart rate accelerated and her cold hands filled with sweat.

'Jo, are you all right? You don't look too good.'

173

The wheel stopped with their passenger-car at the top, and she wanted to cry.

'I don't like it, Josh. I want to get off.'

'Okay, Jo. It's nearly over. We're on our way down in a sec. Look at me.'

Her eyes were darting everywhere. She couldn't focus because she couldn't breathe properly.

'Jo. Look at me.'

Her knuckles had turned white from gripping the metal safety bar so tightly. 'Get me off this thing. Please.'

Josh cupped his gloved hands around her face, forcing her to look directly at him. 'Jo, listen to me. I want you to close your eyes.'

Her tears started to build.

'Jo. Close your eyes.' His voice was soft but firm.

She did as he asked.

'Listen to my voice,' he told her. 'We're sitting on a beach. The sun is shining. It's a beautiful day. The ocean is gently lapping against the shore. Rolls of white foam splash over our toes, and it feels so refreshing. I'm holding your hand, and my other hand is showing you a seashell I picked out of the cool white sand. It's a pearly pink colour, with ridge marks that you're stroking your fingertip over. I'm telling you that there is magic inside, installed by a mermaid. You can smell the sea and taste the salt on your lips, and you're smiling because you know that mermaid. You look out to the clear water, and she's there in the near distance. She's waving at you. Telling you she loves you. That you are safe. You are surrounded by her magic, and she would never let anything happen to you. Just like that, you know you are fine. You are in complete control of your thoughts and feelings. You are the bravest, strongest person in the whole world, and you are happy. So happy. Your mind is relaxed.

Your heartbeat is steady. Your body is being held by the magic of pure, untouched, unconditional love. I rest your head upon my shoulder, and we close our eyes and listen to the ocean breathing. In and out. In and out.'

Joey could see the waves curling over to greet the sand. The soft whooshing noise filled her ears. Her breathing slowed and her hands warmed. A tingling sensation sat beneath her skin. It felt as though love itself was actually touching her. A weightlessness that made no sense created a feeling of safety. There was an energy that entered her, held her, and gave her freedom. She believed in the magic of the mermaid's seashell because she felt she was living inside its enchantment.

'You can open your eyes now,' whispered Josh.

She slowly opened her eyes to see that Josh was still holding her face, the Ferris wheel had gone full circle, and the safety bar had been raised.

His bright eyes held nothing but empathy. 'Why don't we go and get you a cup of tea.'

27

Josh

Josh felt a calmness encircle him as he walked around the noisy, bright funfair. Joey was on his arm, with her head resting on his shoulder. She was quietly sipping a cup of tea from a polystyrene cup. Her hands were steady and warm under his gloves, and her body was relaxed against his. He led her to a wooden bench over by the portable toilets at the quieter end of the fair and sat down. Her body naturally adjusted to his as he leaned back. He tugged her red woolly hat so that her exposed ear was covered.

'Do you want to go home yet, Jo?'

'No.'

'We'll have to get your panda back off Jake at some point.'

'Okay.'

'Let me take you home and put you to bed.'

'No.'

He shifted his body, forcing her to sit up straight. He tried to catch her eyes, but she was staring into her tea.

What can I do to cheer her up? What will make her feel better?

'Hey.' He brushed his hand over her cheek. 'What should we do next?'

Her mouth opened, then closed quickly.

He watched her with concern.

'I'm sorry I ruined today for you, Josh. It was your first time here as well.'

That's what you're thinking?

'You haven't ruined anything. I'm having a great time. I got to bash Jake in a bumper car. I won you a panda bear. I went on a curly whirly slide. I've had you by my side all day.'

She smiled. Weak, but a smile.

That's better. Right, let's make that smile even bigger.

'This one time, in Canada, Jake left me at the top of this steep ski slope. I was terrified. He didn't do it on purpose. He thought I was okay. I thought I could do it, but I was kidding myself. I wasn't ready. I just froze. To this day, I still don't know how long I stayed there for. Jake had to come and rescue me in the end. I felt like such an idiot, and I thought Jake was disappointed, but he was just worried. He told me it was just a blip, and that it wasn't worth any more brainpower, and then he took me ice-skating to remind me of the things I could do.'

Joey's sorrowful eyes brightened. 'How old were you then?'

'Twelve.'

She laughed. 'Twelve!'

'Hey, it doesn't matter how old you are. A blip is a blip.'

'So, you're good at ice-skating, are you?'

He shrugged. 'I'm a better skier. Don't let twelve-year-old Josh fool you.'

Her face filled with a healthy glow.

You look radiant, Jo. I could kiss you right now, but I won't. That's not what you need from me at the moment.

'So, my blip hasn't ruined the day then?' she asked sheepishly.

'Nah. Hang out with me long enough. I'll give your blip a run for its money.'

She giggled. 'Are we having a blip contest?'

Josh waved one hand in the air. 'Are you kidding me. I would win that hands down. I'm made of blips. Blip is my middle name. Of all the blips in the world, I am the biggest blip.'

Joey grabbed his waving hand. 'Okay. I get it.'

He loved that she was laughing. He had done that, and it made him feel good. He liked making her happy.

She gazed around the fair. 'I guess I need to find my own ice rink, then.'

He followed her twinkling eyes. 'What's your Olympic sport, Joey Walker?'

Her head snuggled down into her black scarf. 'The carousel.'

'Oh, you like that do you? Have you seen the film?' He started to sing a song from the movie.

Joey snorted a laugh. 'You like musicals?'

'I like all movies. Gran and I watched loads together, from musicals to martial arts. I was more the musicals, she was the martial arts.'

She laughed, obviously thinking of Edith. 'I like musicals too.'

'Well, that's something we have in common.'

She wrinkled her nose as she tossed her cup into the black bin beside the bench. 'I didn't think we had much in common, if I'm honest.'

'Why did you think that?'

She waved her palm out towards him. 'Well, you know.'

He pursed his lips and shook his head. 'You know what?'

She hesitated.

'Spit it out, Jo.'

'It's just... well, you're Rolex, and I'm more Swatch watch. You're Magnum, and I'm knickerbocker glory. You're Dubai, and I'm Diagon Alley...'

178

'Whoa! Just a minute. Firstly, Jake is the Rolex man. I happen to have a nice collection of Swatch watches, thank you very much. I think they're very artistic. Secondly, I'll have you know that I once ate the biggest knickerbocker glory in the world. Well, that's what it said they sold in the shop window, and as for Diagon Alley. Huh! If I could go there, trust me when I tell you, I would one-hundred-percent go there over Dubai any day of the week.'

Joey bit in her lip as she smiled widely at him.

He nudged her arm. 'This is strictly between you and me though.'

'Why? What's wrong? Don't you want anyone knowing you're a Harry Potter fan?'

He frowned in amusement. 'I'm fine with people knowing that. I just don't want them to think I'm a greedy pig for eating the world's largest knickerbocker glory.'

Joey burst out laughing.

He stood and offered his hand. 'My lady, your horse awaits.'

She took his hand, and he gently kissed her glove.

'Do you want your gloves back now?' she asked.

'You keep them on. My hands are warm.'

They quietly made their way towards the carousel.

'Thanks, Josh.'

'What for?'

She smiled, pressing her mouth into his arm. 'Being the world's biggest blip.'

'Hey, someone has to hold the title.'

* * *

On the way home, Josh steered his motorbike off the main road and up a country lane that led towards Wishing Point.

He felt Joey tap his chest. He knew she would be curious about his detour. He pulled over onto a semicircle mound of dirt and turned off the engine.

The last time he had brought her to that exact spot, they had walked over into the long grass to their right and he had made love to her under the stars. He wasn't there for that this time. He just wanted her to remember that moment. He wanted her to feel connected to him the same way he felt connected to her.

All of the feelings associated to that time were rushing through him. He removed his helmet and looked away from the grass to stare down at the lit-up view of Sandly. He took a deep breath, inhaling the smell of night-time.

Joey shifted behind him. She climbed off the back of the bike and lifted her helmet.

He looked over his shoulder at her. 'Do you want to go further up to Wishing Point?'

She shook her head. 'No. It's nice here. I've always liked this view of a night.'

I know.

He placed his helmet on the handlebar and slid back on the seat.

Joey walked around to the front of his red bike, placed her helmet on the other handlebar, and climbed on the front of the seat, facing him.

Josh was overcome with nostalgia. There had been many times when she sat on his bike that way. Each time filled him with desire for her.

She ran her fingers through her hair as she tipped her head backwards. 'What made you want to come up here?'

Do you actually know what you're doing to me right now?

He waited until she lowered her head to look at him. He swallowed down the breath caught in his dry throat. 'Didn't want to go home just yet.'

'It's cold up here.'

He held open his arms, offering her the warmth of a cuddle.

Joey shuffled forward and sank into his chest.

Balancing himself, he closed his eyes, holding on to the moment.

He felt her giggle.

'Do you remember that time in the grass over there?'

He opened his eyes and smiled to himself. 'Yeah, I remember.'

'We were a lot younger then.'

'It was a lot warmer that night.'

He felt her lift her head, and her nose nuzzle the side of his ear.

'I think we made our own heat,' she whispered playfully.

He laughed through his nose.

Oh, we're going to again in a minute if you keep that up.

Their bodies stilled for a moment.

He tapped her back. 'Turn around, Jo. You're missing the view.'

She loosened her arms and twisted on the seat, guided by his hands. She rested her back on his chest and put her feet up on the bike.

Josh leaned closer to her, placing his arms around her knees. His face was touching hers as they quietly stared down at the lights.

'Where's your favourite place?' she asked. 'You've been so many places.'

Josh started to sing "In My Life", by The Beatles. He stopped singing and slightly nudged her head. 'Pepper Bay is my favourite place. It's always felt like home.'

Being with you is my favourite place, but if I say that out loud, I'll just sound corny.

'I'd like to visit more places.'

'I can show you the world, if you want, Jo.'

She muffled her laugh. 'You sound like Aladdin.'

'Well, I don't have a magic carpet, but I do have a private plane.'

'Yeah, but you don't have a genie.'

He moved his head so that his lips were resting on her cheek. 'I am the genie.'

She turned slightly so that her mouth was closer to his. 'How many wishes do I get?'

A hint of a smirk hit his mouth. 'All of them.'

28

Joey

Joey woke, her head resting on Josh's bare chest. She looked over the top of him at the cold fireplace and the large panda bear sitting beside it. She placed her head back down upon him and smiled because they were in the bed on the living room floor inside Honeybee Cottage. A sense of belonging filled her. She really wanted it to be her forever home, but she hadn't told him yet.

He let out a contented moan as his arm tightened around her, pulling her body closer to his. 'Morning, Jo.'

She stared at her hand on his chest. 'Morning. You slept well last night.'

'I always sleep well when you're with me.'

She rolled her head up to see his sleepy face smile her way.

'We need a two-week plan,' he told her.

'What do you mean?'

'I say, for the next two weeks, just to start with, we go shopping and buy some furniture.'

Joey smiled to herself and lowered her head.

'What do you think?' he asked.

'Sounds like a good plan.'

She felt him kiss her head.

I don't know if I should do this. Buying furniture. Setting up home. Something doesn't feel right. He feels right. The cottage feels right, but... oh, I don't know. I love him. I'm not losing him. I'm just going to do it.

She sat up and looked down at him. 'Do you like decorating?'

'I don't know. I've never done it. How about you?'

'I've never done it either. Nate does everything like that at the farm.'

'We can hire people. They'll know what they're doing, and we need to get that kitchen sorted.'

'What's wrong with the kitchen?'

'It's not the one you want.'

Joey smiled. 'I know the one I want. It's in my vision book.'

Josh shuffled his body up. Faint lines appeared around his mouth. 'You have a vision book?'

'I've been planning my home for years.'

'This I have to see.'

She nudged him in the ribs. 'It's got some good stuff in it, I'll have you know. I'm just not sure how to bring it all together, that's all.'

'Leave that to me. I know the perfect person for the job. Her name's Jazz, and she does this sort of thing for a living. I'll call her, bring her over.'

Jazz? What if she's someone he's slept with? I don't want anyone from his back catalogue here. What can I say? I can't just ask him if he has slept with her.

'How do you know her?'

'She went to the same university as me.'

That doesn't answer my question.

'Were you close?'

He climbed out of bed, stretching his back and clicking his neck. 'Yeah. We got on really well. You'll like her.'

Will I?

* * *

Within three hours of Josh calling his interior designer friend, she was standing in Honeybee Cottage humming into Joey's vision book.

Joey watched her with eyes wide as the pages of her large purple book were slowly flipped back and forth. She felt a touch violated as though the elegant woman was reading her diary.

My God, would you look at her. She looks like a movie star. I wish I had cheekbones like that. I wonder if she uses lip filler. She looks like she works out. Maybe her body isn't natural. Perhaps her rich dad gifted her cosmetic surgery for her eighteenth birthday or something. Please tell me Josh didn't sleep with her. I can't cope if she's an ex-girlfriend. I wish she'd say something about my ideas. What is that she's humming? Josh is watching her. What's he thinking? If only my brain worked earlier on. I could have put a stop to this. Who comes at a click of a finger anyway? Oh, I'm fed up. I don't want her here. Why did he have to pick her? I should have spoken to Jake. I bet he knows someone else. Someone other than Little Miss Flawless Halle Berry.

Jazz raised her head. Her perfect loose curls bounced slightly on her shoulders. 'I like this, Joey. I can make this work. You'll have your dream kitchen within three weeks.' She looked over at Josh.

He gave a half-shrug and a smile.

Joey's eyes flittered between Josh and Jazz. 'Erm… three weeks?'

Jazz nodded as she straightened up. 'My team will start work first thing tomorrow morning.'

Is she asking me or telling me?

Josh seemed happy enough.

Jazz tucked the vision book under her arm and pulled a small laptop out of her large black bag and started to tap on the keyboard. 'Can I keep this book for now, Joey?'

Joey didn't want her to take it, but Josh was smiling and nodding her way, so she felt she had little choice. 'Erm, okay.'

'I'll be back tomorrow,' said Jazz, putting her laptop away. She reached out her hand to professionally shake Joey's. 'It was lovely to meet you, Joey. Short but sweet, I know, but I have work to do.'

'Oh, you don't have to rush on our account. We can wait, or I'm sure we can find someone else if you're up to your neck in it. Josh shouldn't have bothered you. I know what it's like to be snowed under at work...'

Jazz interrupted, 'Yes, you make lollipops, I hear. That's interesting.'

'I...'

'I'm definitely going to try one,' she added quickly. 'How fabulous. Bespoke candy. I hear they have tiny flowers in them. How quaint. I'll take a batch for my gift baskets. I leave my clients a few treats once I'm finished in their home.'

Josh was grinning widely at Joey.

Joey crossed her arms, then quickly uncrossed them. She shifted her body weight onto her back foot. 'Oh, erm, okay. Thank you.'

Jazz tossed her designer bag over her shoulder and rubbed Joey on the arm as she passed her by in the hallway.

'I'll walk you back to your boat,' said Josh, opening the door.

Do all his friends have private boats and planes?

'Thank you, Josh,' she said smoothly. She glanced back at Joey. 'I left my husband sitting at the wheel. I did promise him I wouldn't be long. Hopefully, he hasn't buggered off somewhere. He did have his eye on those adorable beach huts in the seaside town next door.'

'Sandly,' said Josh.

'We'll visit another time,' said Jazz. 'I like this place. It's full of character and such beauty. I can see why you fell in love, Josh.'

She looked at me when she said that.

Joey waved goodbye as Josh led his old friend outside.

What the hell just happened? One minute, Josh is talking about buying furniture, then I'm bringing my vision book here, and then Jazz the home stylist arrives, flies round the cottage like the Tasmanian Devil, studies my book of ideas, orders a batch of my lollipops, then sails away on her private boat with her, unmentioned until three seconds ago, husband.

29

Josh

During the three weeks it took for Jazz's team of workers to redesign the kitchen, decorate the whole house, and install a new bathroom suite, Josh had sorted out the cabin at the bottom of the garden and arranged all his art equipment. He was glad of the space and the peace and quiet. The cottage had been awash with people, day and night. He had taken to sleeping at the flat with Joey just to get away from the chaos. Plus, he could see it was stressing her. She was baking way more cakes than was needed at the shop, which was always quiet until spring.

Josh knew that Joey could just go home and he could stay at Starlight with Jake and Anna, but he didn't want to feel so far away from her. He had no idea what he was going to do when they moved into Honeybee and they had their own rooms and started their new housemate life. A part of him didn't want that time to arrive.

Each night, Joey had slept by his side. She held him, soothed him, and helped him to sleep. Not once had he woken in a sweat. He hadn't needed to call Rusty for guidance again, as his mind was occupied with all the work that was going on in the cottage. Plus, he also knew that his stability was down to Joey and Pepper Bay.

He placed a blank canvas upon an easel and stared absentmindedly at its texture. No picture came to mind, just Joey. He smiled to himself as he remembered how jealous she had looked when she walked into the bedroom to see him sharing a joke with Jazz. He had casually explained that night how Jazz was his friend's girlfriend at uni, and it seemed to take the edge off the foul atmosphere in the flat. She still held him in bed, and her envious mood fed him some hope.

Joey stood in the doorway. 'I can't believe it's all over. It's been like DIY SOS around here. Peace and quiet at last. No more workers traipsing all over our home. I'm still astonished Jazz completed everything she said she would in three weeks. She's amazing, and she left us a rather nice peach bath bomb in her gift basket. I did ask her for an invoice, but she flat-out refused to show me how much everything cost, which I know is down to you.'

He waved her over to him and placed his arm around her shoulder. 'Call it a moving-in gift.'

'I haven't bought you anything.'

'You can share that bath bomb with me in our new bath.'

She laughed and tilted her head onto him. 'Josh, how am I ever going to pay you back for any of this?'

'I just told you.'

She tapped his chest. 'I'm serious. All this money. The cottage. The decorating. I can't afford any of it.'

'You will soon, when you've sold a zillion lollipops. You'll be the next Willy Wonka.'

'He's a character in a book.'

'It's done now, anyway. We did it. We got Honeybee just how you want it, and now...' He stopped.

'Now what?'

'We can move in.' His voice was slightly broken, and he knew that she had picked up on that.

Joey moved herself around so that she was standing in front of him. 'What's wrong, Josh? You don't sound happy.'

I'm not happy, but I'm not saying anything to you about how I feel. I just can't bring myself to have this conversation with you. I feel too tired for this right now. Living with you should be a time to celebrate, but instead... I don't know.

'I'm okay,' he lied.

Her eyes widened as her brow lifted.

He had to say something. 'It's just new, isn't it? You, me, living together. Obviously, not together, together, but you know, sharing a house.'

She took a step back. 'We don't have to go through with this if you don't feel ready.'

He moved towards her. 'I'm ready, Jo.'

'That's good, because I've already unpacked my things.'

He watched her as she stopped at the door.

'Josh.'

'Yeah?'

'Do you think we're weird?'

He breathed out a laugh through his nose. 'Weird? Why would you say that?'

She scrunched one shoulder to her jaw. 'I think people might think that about us. You know, how we are with each other.'

'I don't care what they think. It's none of their business.' He realised his tone sounded a little irate. He cleared his throat and lowered his eyes submissively. 'I only care about what you think.'

'I think we're just us. I know we don't have a normal friendship, not that normal really exists, and how do we know what goes on in the lives of others, but I sometimes wonder if people talk about us. Sometimes I wonder if we should talk about us.'

Josh's eyes narrowed. 'What do you want to talk about?'

'I think we should stick to our own bedrooms now that we're house sharing. One day, we're going to meet other people, and they won't like how close we are, so perhaps we should give us, our friendship, some boundaries now. That way, we'll be more prepared when that time comes. We'll be more like normal people.'

His brow tightened and his nostrils flared. 'I don't want to be like normal people. I like the way things are. I'm not planning on meeting anyone anyway.'

'But you will one day.'

'How do you know?'

She shrugged. 'That's life.'

'Fine. If you want me to back off. I will.'

His bright eyes glossed over as she left the cabin.

What the hell was that? What did I do? Where did that even come from? Has she met someone else? She can't have. I would know. Someone would know. This is a small place. You can't hide anything here. Maybe I'm just being too much. I keep touching her. I sleep by her side. Maybe she needs a break from me and my demon. She shouldn't be on the nightshift anyway. It's not her problem. It's mine. She shouldn't have to deal with it. It'll be okay. She just needs a break. That's what it is. That's fair enough. I'll be all right. I'll meditate before bed. That helps. I'll do some yoga. Wind down. I'll be fine. We'll be fine.

He jumped out of his train of thought as Joey came back to the door.

'Josh, I want you to know that even though it's right for us to have our own rooms, if you ever need me to help you sleep, I'll always be there. Nothing's changed with that. I'd never leave you suffering. I'll always hold you when you need me.' She shook her head and tightened her eyes as though angry at herself. 'I want you to tell me when you need me.'

I need you right now.

Josh controlled the unsteady breath that was trying to escape his mouth. 'Okay.'

Joey swallowed hard. Her hands were fidgeting in front of her. 'We don't have to have separate rooms tonight. You know, what with it being our first proper night here, and you sleeping in a new room. I could join you until you're used to your new space. I know you sleep better when you're used to a place. I don't know. It's just a suggestion. You're doing so well. I don't want anything to set you back.'

Is she feeling guilty? Does she think she has to do this?

'I'll be okay, but thanks, Jo. I'm a big boy now. I think I can handle it.'

'We both know night terrors aren't about age.' She folded her arms in a huff. 'You really suffer when you're stressed, and a new place could stress you.'

'I'll just have a drop of scotch if I get too stressed.'

She didn't laugh at his poor attempt at a joke. 'That's not funny, Josh.'

He sighed inwardly. 'It's fine, Jo. I'll be okay.'

'You promise to bang on the wall if you need me?'

He forced a smile. 'I promise.'

30

Joey

The air was cool and smelled like fresh paint. There was no sound coming from outside or in the cottage. Joey had been tossing and turning for three hours. Her eyes were wide awake and her chest was tight, annoying her breathing. She slapped her hands on her peach duvet and shuffled up to a sitting position, glancing over at the silver digital clock on the oak bedside cabinet.

It's two o'clock in the bloody morning. Good thing I don't have to be in the shop tomorrow until late. I'm getting annoyed now.

She punched the plump pillow behind her and then glanced at the vacant one by her side.

He'll be all right. He's probably fast asleep. Maybe I should look in on him. No, that's just stupid. He should be here with me. Why did I have to suggest separate rooms? I think it annoyed him. He didn't look too pleased about the idea. I've got to stop saying things that go against how I feel. This is ridiculous. Oh, I can't breathe properly now. This is getting on my nerves.

She tossed the cover off her in one sharp movement. The night-time air flowed through her green flannel pyjamas as she made her way over to the opened window. Closing her eyes, she deeply inhaled the night, trying to fill her lungs.

A light in the cabin caught her eyes as soon as she opened them. She could see Josh through the building's glass door. He was wearing dark shorts and a white tee-shirt that had a big rip from the neckline down to the top of his chest. She knew that top well. He'd had it for years. She was the one who had ripped it during a moment of passion they had shared in the swimming pool at Starlight Cottage. She smiled to herself at the memory, then homed in on his face. He had his glasses on and was sitting in front of an easel, painting something. He looked peaceful, content.

Every memory I have of us together is filled with happiness. He makes my heart smile. I can't not be with him. He's a part of me. There's nothing I can do about it. I can see that now. He will never leave my heart. He's everything to me. He's eternity.

A wave of love swept over her body. Butterflies filled her stomach and a warmth settled in her eyes. Before she had time to explore her thoughts and feelings any further, she was standing inside the cosy cabin.

Josh turned his head and glanced up at her over the top of his glasses. He had a paintbrush resting sideways in his teeth, which he slowly removed before looking back at the painting.

Joey didn't even feel her bare feet move, but somehow they had led her towards him. She lifted her leg over both of his and straddled his lap, facing him. She wrapped her arms around his neck and lowered her head. The tightness in her chest loosened, allowing her to breathe freely again. She felt Josh's arm movements. One hand rested on her back, and the other continued to gently sweep his paintbrush over the canvas board.

The old-fashioned record player sitting in the corner of the room had finished playing a song, and another vinyl was waiting to fall down on top of the record.

Joey watched the small, blue, suitcase-looking contraption with curiosity, wondering what the next song would be.

Edith Reynolds had a vast collection of records from the 1950s and 1960s. She loved that old record player, and she passed on her love of music to her grandson.

The record dropped, making Joey blink, and the slow velvety sound of Johnny Mathis filled the room as he started singing "Chances Are".

Josh joined in, quietly singing along.

There were many things about Josh that stirred something inside Joey. She loved his hands, his forearms, the back of his neck, when he wore his glasses, and especially when he sang. The softness in his voice when he relaxed, not trying to own the music, was one of her favourite sounds. His laidback demeanour to the lyrics of a love song melted her heart, warmed her soul, and stoked the fire within her that burned only for him.

She moved her head and tenderly kissed his neck. She only planned the one kiss, but she did it again, and again, unable to stop. Not wanting to stop. His warm skin against her lips tasted sweet and salty, and his fresh scent reached the deepest parts of her soul. Her breath wasn't leaving her mouth. It stayed down deep, holding her heart.

Josh stopped singing, as his body stilled for a second. He slowly lowered his paintbrush, then pressed his head against hers, moving with her gentle motion until his mouth met her lips.

A hushed gasp vibrated onto her as she cupped his warm face in her cool hands and arched her back whilst his tongue entered her mouth.

His hands held on to her back, pulling her closer into his chest. His head dipped, and he kissed down her neck as she raised her head towards the white lights above her.

She closed her eyes and allowed herself to get lost in every soft and gentle touch. Her heart stirred as his fingers touched her top and slowly unfastened one button at a time. She looked back down and tightened her grip on his tee-shirt. He relaxed his arms so that she could raise it up over his head with ease.

He stood, carrying her with him, and reached out to a wicker chair behind them to pull off the blue blanket and matching cushion that were sitting there. He carefully lowered her to the wooden floor.

Joey clung on to his strong body as the blanket fell down into a creased slump behind her. She placed her head on the cushion that was manoeuvred beneath her neck and looked into the azure-blue eyes watching her.

Josh lowered his body over hers and kissed her lips. He was steady and slow as he made his way down over her collarbone and further down towards her stomach. He lifted himself and looked up into her eyes.

She raised her hips, allowing him to remove her bottoms. She took control of the air leaving her mouth as his lips met with the inside of her thigh. She watched him take off his shorts and make his way back up to gaze down at her face. He reached up to remove his glasses, but she stopped him. His fingers stroked over her knuckles, then came down to rest on her cheek to gently wipe away a teardrop that had made an appearance.

'You okay?' he whispered.

Joey's smile reached her eyes. 'Yeah.'

He lowered his face and affectionately kissed her damp cheek. 'You sure?'

'Yeah.' She ran her fingers through his dark hair and waited for his mouth to return to hers. Every part of her softened beneath him.

A faint crease appeared on his brow as he pulled his face back to look at her. She mimicked his expression, causing a smile to hit his eyes before he kissed the tip of her nose.

All of her love for him surged through her whole body to settle in her eyes. She slowly traced the outline of his mouth with her attentive gaze. It was as though she had been hypnotised by his aura, because her body felt in a state of tranquil bliss.

'One sec,' he whispered.

She watched him quickly lean over to a drawer and remove a small silver wrapper.

'You have condoms in your art drawer?'

He smiled softly as he ripped the wrapper open. 'I've put them everywhere in case we ever...' He stopped talking, looking slightly lost.

Joey brushed her lips over his, pulling him closer to her. His warm breath tingled her skin. She quietly gasped and pushed her head deeper into the soft cushion as he connected their bodies in every way. Josh's mouth was on her neck, whispering her name as the music stopped. Their in-sync motion continued to move to the silent song that only they could hear inside their hearts.

31

Josh

A small brown bird landed on the bedroom windowsill, looking inside at the man sitting up in bed. Josh watched it twitch its head and open its mouth as though silently speaking to him. His eyes rolled down to stare at the back of Joey's head. She was still sleeping, curled on her side, oblivious to his early-morning thoughts.

He closed his eyes for a few seconds and controlled the heavy breath weighing down his lungs.

I can't believe I did that. What was I thinking? I feel like crap.

He opened his eyes and tilted his head towards his lap. He didn't even have the energy to fight back the disappointment flooding through him.

I was doing so well. We were doing so well. I've just taken us straight back to square one. I've ruined everything. I need to speak to Rusty.

He got out of bed and quietly left Joey's room. He made his way into his bedroom, grabbed his phone off the bedside cabinet, pulled on a pair of pyjama bottoms, and headed to the bathroom and closed and locked the door. The toilet seat was already down, so he sat there to call his mentor.

'Hey, Josh. You're calling late. I was just about to go to bed.' Rusty's voice held a soft tone.

'I'm sorry. I keep forgetting about the time difference in New York.'

'That's okay. What's wrong? You sound fatigued.'

Josh leaned one arm forward to rest on his knee. His hand pushed against his weary head. 'I broke my celibacy.'

'How many times?'

The image of Joey lying beneath him on the blanket inside the cabin entered his mind. He watched himself carry her naked body back to the cottage. She had her legs wrapped around his waist and the blue blanket wrapped around them both. They had spent so long making love in her bed, he had lost all concept of time. The memory churned warmth into his stomach and regret into his mind.

'Twice,' he replied.

'Different women?' asked Rusty, no trace of judgment in his voice.

Josh moved his head in his hand. 'With Joey.'

'Oh, okay.'

'I feel like shit, Rusty. I've put us right back to how we used to be.'

'Why do you think that?'

'It's all we used to do whenever I was here. You know that. I've just recreated it. I wanted things to be different this time.'

'Things are different this time, Josh.'

Josh raised his head. 'How are they?'

Rusty's voice remained soft and calm. 'Because, Josh, you didn't jump into bed with her the first day you arrived, nor the second day, nor the third. You have spent time getting to know each other instead. Relationships aren't built on sex. They're deeper than that. You're showing her a different side to yourself. You love her very much, and she loves you too.'

Josh wasn't sure about that.

'I'm not sure how she feels about me, if I'm honest. One minute, I do, and then I don't.'

'Josh, she has spent practically every day by your side. She holds you in bed. She listens when you have something to say. She wears the ring you gave her on her wedding finger. She has moved in with you. She can't keep away from you, just as much as you can't keep away from her. I'm telling you, she loves you. Why don't you be honest with her now. Tell her what's in your heart.'

Josh sighed. 'When you say it, it sounds so simple, but when I look at her, it's not. I'm back to being her summer romance, all because I couldn't get a grip.'

Argh! It's so frustrating.

'Josh, what did we learn about love?'

He looked over at the white oval bath. 'That it messes us up.'

Rusty laughed quietly. 'Come on, dig deep.'

'We overcomplicate the emotion by adding in our fears. Well, I do.'

He visualised Rusty slowly nodding whilst twiddling with his copper-coloured beard, as he often did.

'Josh, you have come so far in your journey of self-discovery. You can't allow your fears to represent themselves as failures.'

'But I feel like a failure. I feel as though I should be handing back my sobriety chip or something.'

'You didn't go off and party with random girls, Josh. You made love to the woman you are in love with. You don't need to hand back any chips. What you did was inevitable. It was just a matter of time. Sure, you wanted to wait longer. I get that, but it has happened now. Now is the time not to dwell. It is the time to move forward.'

Josh's eyes widened. 'Move forward? I don't know how to move forward from last night. I don't know what to say to her. I don't think I can look at her right now. Right now, I want to run away. I want to come back to New York.'

'When I first met you, you told me that you were tired of running away. What we have achieved is you facing your darkness. You know now it's how we learn about ourselves. We can't hide from life, Josh. We have to look it straight in the eye and search for the lesson. Search for light in the dark. Search for the truth that is being revealed to us. If we run, we see nothing. We learn nothing. We achieve nothing.'

'I don't feel as though I have achieved anything.'

'You have achieved plenty, Josh. Not only did you go back there to be with your brother, you helped him say goodbye to your grandfather. You have grown closer to Joey, and you planted roots. You have hardly called me. Okay, you update me with texts, but you're not heavily relying on me. You haven't had a drink even though you wanted to, and you finally know what you want for your life. I know you're scared. We're all scared. Don't be fooled by those who appear to have their shit together. The reality is, it's a scary world, and our perspective can make or break us. You're coming at this from the wrong angle.'

'I'm looking at all the negatives, and by doing so, I'm blocking out the positive.'

'That's right.'

Josh glanced up at the ceiling. The weight on his shoulders was starting to disperse, but his heart was still agonising over his next move with Joey. 'I still don't know what to do.'

'You're changing, Josh. And change in a person doesn't happen overnight. There are many of your old traits pulling you back. You have to think about the person you want to be, not the person you're used to. All your life, you have loved this woman, from your teenage years to today. If you run away from her again, you might never return. Isn't she worth fighting for? Isn't the new you worth fighting for?'

Josh swallowed hard. He knew full well he was scared that he was going to run. He didn't want to run away. He was fed up with that action. 'I just don't know how to handle today.'

'That's because your old self is calling the shots. As we know, old habits die hard. I know what your mind is telling you, but what is your heart saying?'

'Don't run.'

'Anything else?'

Josh raked his hand through his dishevelled hair whilst frowning. 'The same thing it always says, I guess.'

'Which is?'

'That I love her.'

'Is that so hard to do?'

'When it's one-sided, yes.'

'But it's not, Josh.'

'I admire your optimism, Rusty, but you can't really know how she feels.'

'Close your eyes, Josh.'

Josh didn't question him. He immediately did as he was told.

'Now, I want you to go back to last night,' said Rusty. 'Do not tell me. That's not my business. I want you to remember how her eyes looked. Were they empty? Perhaps despondent. Were they filled with lust, or was it a glossy-eyed look? Did she hold warmth there? Were they focused on you? You will know if you saw any signs of love. Our eyes are the gatekeepers to our soul. Think about it. Remember her eyes, Josh. What story were they telling you?'

Josh was right back there. She was gazing up at him. He wiped away her falling tear, but she wasn't sad. She could feel the same emotion as him. It was overwhelming her. He felt the same way. She stroked his face and kissed him tenderly. There were no signs of lust. Every move was slow and soft. She was loving him. Right there, in that moment, he was so sure she was loving him.

Rusty's voice entered his thoughts. 'Move forward now, Josh. Stick to your plan. It's going to be all right.'

32

Joey

The new cream kitchen did little to spark joy for Joey, who was sitting on a stall leaning on the oak-topped blue kitchen island eating lunch by herself. She hadn't seen Josh all morning. Her bed was cold and empty on his side when she woke up. He didn't even leave her a note or a text, and it made her feel unwanted and used.

I wish last night never happened. Why did I do that to myself? Clearly, it wasn't what I thought. I can't believe he hasn't even spoken to me today. Where the hell is he? Has he left?

She leapt from the seat and sprinted up the stairs, two at a time. She rushed into his bedroom and flung open the door to the small walk-in wardrobe.

All his things are still here. That doesn't matter. He never travels with much. He'll just buy new things wherever he is.

She pulled her phone out from her cardigan pocket.

No. I'm not doing it. I'm not calling him. If he's gone, so be it. I'm not chasing him.

The phone vibrated in her hand, and her eyes lit up as she quickly turned it over to look at the screen. She deflated as Ruby's name flashed before her.

'Hello, Rubes.'

'Where are you? I thought you would be in by now. Molly's gone. She's got dentist, and I keep getting in a right pickle with icing Sharon Laney's birthday cake. Black takes no prisoners, you know. I've wiped it off so many times now, the bloody thing's turned grey.'

Joey slowly closed the door on Josh's clothes. 'Sorry, Ruby. I lost track of time. I've been sorting my kitchen cupboards all morning, seeing what I want where, and then I got hungry. Anyway, I'll be right there. Give me ten minutes. And step away from the black icing. Have your lunch.'

She hung up, finished getting dressed, put on some light makeup, and left for the tea shop.

Pepper Lane was as quiet as ever. The end of January had arrived already, bringing with it an icy chill. Joey made the short, cold walk down to Edith's Tearoom by foot. She was wrapped in her big black coat, red scarf, and red-and-black checked hat. Her hands were firmly tucked into her pockets, and her mind was desperately trying to freeze out Josh Reynolds.

She entered the shop to find Sharon Laney sitting at a table with Ruby, dunking shortbread into her tea.

'Hello, Joey. I've come to pick up my daughter's birthday cake, but Ruby said it's not ready yet.'

Joey felt terrible. She was never late with people's orders, and Sharon was a loyal customer from Sandly.

'I'm so sorry, Sharon. Give me ten minutes to get it ready for you.'

She knew Sharon was a reasonable woman. She was an old school friend of her brother's, but all the same, she had to get her cake ready as soon as possible.

Ruby was right about one thing. The once white fondant was smeared with faded black icing. Joey had no choice, she had to be honest. She picked up the silver board and carried the cake out to the shop.

'I'm very sorry, Sharon. This is what I'm dealing with. I'm afraid it's going to take a little longer than expected. I'm going to have to re-cover the whole thing. Do you want to have lunch while you wait? On us, of course.'

Sharon flicked back her ginger hair as she glanced at the cake.

Ruby recoiled. 'It's my fault. I couldn't get to grips with those straight lines you wanted me to pipe down the sides.'

Sharon smiled, revealing her large white teeth. 'I think it looks quite artistic. What about if you smeared on some dark blue and added silver stars. My daughter loves anything galactic.'

Joey frowned. 'Galactic?'

'Yeah,' said Sharon. 'Make it look like space.'

Joey nodded. 'I can do that. Give me five minutes.'

She took the cake back to the kitchen and got busy with blue icing and star cutters. She sprinkled the cake with edible silver and white glitter and painted over the wording with matching ink, made from silver dust and some water. She knew it would take a while to dry, but as the wording was on the cake board and not the cake, chances were, it would be left alone. She carefully placed the finished product into a white cardboard box, leaving the lid off so that she could show Sharon.

'Ooh, that's lovely, Jo. Well done.'

Ruby was impressed too. 'I'm so sorry. I still feel bad.'

Sharon touched her arm. 'Stop that, Ruby. We all mess up from time to time. Anyway, it all worked out for the best in the end, and I got to have a free ham-and-cheese toastie, so I'm good.'

Joey placed the lid on the box. 'I can knock ten percent off.'

Sharon shook her head. Her laugh lines ran deep as she smiled. 'Don't be daft. I got lunch, didn't I?' She pulled out her Gucci purse and handed over the money.

'Well, I'm never touching black icing again,' said Ruby, taking the money over to the till.

'Practice makes perfect,' said Joey, sitting opposite Sharon.

Sharon looked at Joey whilst waving one hand behind her towards the doorway. 'Have you heard, Dolly's is closing down.'

Joey shook her head. 'No, it's not. Her niece is taking over. She's going to revamp the old place. She's the crafty type. Makes her own candles, that sort of thing.'

Sharon's face lit up. 'Ooh, that'll be nice.'

'Can't believe you're behind with the gossip, Sharon,' called out Ruby from behind the counter.

Sharon reached her hand across the table to Joey. 'Speaking of gossip, what's this I hear about you moving in with Josh Reynolds. That can't be true, surely.'

Joey felt her brow tighten. 'Why do you say it like that?'

'Well, you know what he's like. Bit of a playboy. You're better than that, Jo.'

'We're not together. It's just a temporary arrangement.'

Sharon sat back. A look of relief flashed across her full face of makeup. 'That's good, because I saw him in Sandly as I was leaving. Going into Spiky Rick's.'

So, Josh is still here.

Ruby laughed. 'You still call him that?'

'Listen, he's never going to be allowed to forget that hairdo.'

Joey's hands had started to fidget. 'Obviously, Josh fancied Italian for his lunch today.'

Sharon chuckled. 'That's not all he fancied. Should have seen the woman on his arm. Very glamourous. City type. Tall, blonde, leggy.'

A thump hit Joey straight in the heart.

Ruby leant over the counter. 'Joey's tall, blonde, and leggy.'

Joey looked down at her knees.

Sharon waved her hand in the air. 'Yeah, but Jo's, you know, more relaxed.'

Joey frowned with confusion.

Sharon smiled sympathetically. 'You're lovely, Joey. Much prettier than her. I know. I got a good look. See what I mean about him. He's that flaky type. Don't let him stay with you for too long.'

'She needs to start dating too,' called out Ruby.

Sharon agreed. 'What about Scott Harper. I heard he's back in town.'

Joey shot a glance at Ruby. 'He is? You never said, Rubes.'

'He's keeping himself to himself at the moment.'

Sharon scoffed. 'He needs to spread himself around a bit. I wouldn't say no to Clark Kent.'

Ruby frowned. 'Do you all call him that?'

Sharon nodded at Joey. 'And more, eh, Jo?' She looked over at Ruby. 'Can't you see it, Rubes? He's definitely got that Clark Kent vibe. He's bloody gorgeous. You tell him not to be so shy, Ruby. He can ring me anytime.'

Ruby raised her brow. 'You're not coming near my nephew. You'd eat him alive.'

Sharon agreed. 'Well, that would be the plan. Anyway, he's not a teenager, Ruby. I'm sure he can play with the grown-ups. How old is he now?'

'He's forty-five.'

Sharon's eyes widened. 'Bloody hell! I didn't know he was that old. I only saw him a couple of years back. He looked younger than me.'

Ruby grinned. 'We have youthful genes in my family. Anyway, forty-five isn't old.'

'I just thought he was a lot younger than me. Well, you can still let him know that I'm available.'

'I thought you were trying to set Joey up on a date, not yourself.'

Sharon turned her attention back to Joey. 'If not Clark Kent, what about Monty James or his brother, Wendall. He likes you, Jo. Give him a ring. Arrange dinner or something. Worth a shot. You never know. He might be *The One*.'

Ruby shook her head. 'She's still not talking to Wendall.'

'Make amends,' said Sharon. 'He's an eligible bachelor. He dresses well. Have you noticed that? He always looks as though he's just stepped off the catwalk. He's got a flash car as well. Don't know why he's single. He seems nice enough. Probably got something wrong with him. You might have to look out for red flags. Still, worth a go, Joey. Go on, ask him out.'

Maybe I will, if Josh is off out on dates. Would have thought he might have waited at least a week or something. Talk about cold. Guess that's the only message he wanted to send me. He knows full well that word would get back to me about his leggy blonde. I'm not going to cry. I'm not. I'm going to call Wendall. Josh has made it very clear I'm only good for sex. I thought things were different. At least now I know it was just my imagination going berserk. Okay. There's nothing I can do about this. It is what it is. What it has always been. I've been an idiot. I have to focus now. Create some sort of normal life for myself.

'I'm going to call Wendall,' she announced to Sharon.

'Go on then,' Sharon urged. 'Do it now.'

Okay, I will.

She pulled her phone out of her pocket and called Wendall James.

He sounded wary. 'Hello, Joey. I didn't think I would hear from you again.'

'Well, that's just it, Wendall. You owe me an apology, and you can start by taking me out to dinner tonight. We'll go to Swan Lake, and you're paying. I'll meet you there at six.'

'Erm, okay, Jo. I'll see you there then.'

Joey hung up and smiled triumphantly over at Sharon.

Sharon scrunched up her button nose. 'Well, that's one way to ask someone out.'

33

Josh

Josh was slouched into the plump cream sofa in the living room of Honeybee Cottage. He had been there for over an hour, reading a book by Henry David Thoreau. He had no idea where Joey was. She wasn't home when he got back, and she wasn't in the shop when he popped in at three o'clock. He desperately wanted to talk to her, but she didn't answer his call, and he didn't want to keep calling. It was a conversation he wanted at home anyway. He looked down at his phone on the sofa, hoping it was her. His face dropped when he saw it was Jake.

'Hello, Jake.'

'Have you got a minute?'

'Sure, what's up?'

'It's Scott Harper. He's back, and he has asked Anna if she'll hire him to work in The Book Gallery.'

Josh bobbed his head. 'Makes sense. He's an artist. He's got some of his paintings in there. Plus, he used to work there before, part-time for Betty Blake. It'll be nice to see him again. I'll have to give him a ring.'

'Can we stick to my subject first?'

'What exactly is your subject, Jake?'

'Should I let him work in the shop?'

Josh frowned as he grinned to himself. 'I thought Anna was in charge there.'

'She is, but…'

Josh waited for his brother to finish his sentence, but it didn't sound as though he was going to add to it. He heard him sigh.

'Jake, are you worried about Superman running off with your woman?' He quickly pulled his lips in so that he wouldn't laugh.

'I… Well, no, of course not. Anna loves me. I have full trust in her.'

Josh shook his head. 'So, what's the problem?'

Like I don't know already.

'I don't have a problem. Well, okay, maybe… Okay, I do have a problem with it. There, happy now, I said it.'

'So, don't hire him.'

'I can't do that. He's a perfect fit for the place. He'll come in handy when I want to take Anna away on holiday, which I'll be doing soon. I plan on taking her to see a lot of the world.'

'Jake, seriously, I wouldn't worry about Scott. He's always been a decent person. He's our friend. Plus, you know how quiet he is. I don't think he's got it in him to hit on anyone.'

'He doesn't need to hit on anyone. He's Superman.'

Josh laughed quietly. 'Just hire him. Anna loves you. Any fool can see that. You're safe.'

'I can't lose her, Josh. You don't know what that thought feels like.'

Yeah, I do.

'Tell Anna about your insecurities.'

'I did.'

'And?'

'It amused her.'

It is funny.

212

'I'm sure she won't hire him if it makes you feel that bad, Jake.'

'She did say that, but I feel bad towards Scott as well. That's why I called you. I was hoping you would be more helpful. I bet you laughed.'

Josh was trying hard not to. 'No, not me.'

'Well, what would you do in my position?'

'Firstly, I would be grateful I'm with the woman I love, then I'd trust her to make the right decisions for our relationship. Anna working with Scott will be okay, Jake. I wouldn't mind, but you're practically glued to her hip all day anyway. Just breathe. You can't let this stress you. You're in a good place now, and everything will be all right. She loves you. She's not going anywhere. Just remember how you met, everything she has said to you, and believe in her. Believe in your future together. You have big plans.'

Jake took a deep breath that caused a rumble in the phone. 'You're right.'

Josh raised his eyebrows in surprise. 'You want to say that again, because I don't think you say that to me very often.'

'I said, you're right. Don't push it.'

Josh lifted one hand up, surrendering. 'Okay.' He smiled down the phone. 'Go and tell Anna how much you love her, and I'll speak to you later.'

'I'm taking her out for dinner tonight. Do you want to join us?'

'No, I'm good, thanks. Enjoy.' He hung up and shook his head.

The front door opened, and Joey walked in holding a large carrier bag in her arms. She didn't stop to say hello. She went straight upstairs.

Josh wasn't entirely sure if she had even noticed him.

I'll wait till she comes back down.

213

He glanced at his red-and-white flecked watch.

Half five. Maybe I should cook dinner. I'll wait. See what she says.

He went back to reading and didn't glance up until she appeared in front of him. His eyes curiously rolled up to peer over the top of his glasses.

Joey was wearing matching black lace underwear. She had extra makeup on, the bottom of her hair was curled, and she was holding a dress in each hand.

'Which do you think I should wear?' she asked.

He looked at the sleek black one to her left, then over to the ribbed dark-blue one to her right. His eyes rolled up to meet her deadpan expression.

She held the black dress in front of her and quickly switched to the blue. 'Well?'

'Erm… what's it for?'

Avoiding eye contact, she swiftly replied, 'Swan Lake. It's a restaurant over by…'

'I know where it is.'

Her eyes glared at him. 'Of course you do.'

Josh could sense some tension. 'When are you going there?'

'Right now.' She wiggled the dresses.

'Who with?'

'Not that it's any of your business, but I have a date.'

Whoa! Where did that come from?

He swallowed his anger and remained perfectly still, struggling not to blink. He relaxed his clenched jaw because he had the same question to ask and didn't want to spit it out at her. 'Who with?'

She glanced down at the black dress. The hostility in her face had been replaced by nonchalance. 'Wendall.'

Wendall James? Is she kidding me?

'Since when?' was all he could manage.

She was still staring at the short black dress. 'Since earlier on today.'

Josh lowered his book onto his lap because his fingers were turning white from his tight grip.

'I think the blue,' she said casually.

Wait, let me get this straight. You make love to me last night, and now tonight you're going out with Wendall James. Smooth as velvet Wendall James. Wendall James, with his picture-perfect Instagram life. You're wearing underwear that I've never seen before, and where the hell did those dresses come from? He's going to see you like that. Is that underwear for him? Why are you doing this to me? I thought you had real feelings for me. How could I have got this so wrong? I saw it. It was in her eyes, just like Rusty said. She was loving me. What the hell is she doing to me now? Why are you doing this, Jo?

He watched her walk away over to the doorway where she proceeded to shuffle her slim body into the little blue outfit. She flicked her hair and slipped her feet into shiny black heels.

Josh had never seen Joey look so elegant before. He was used to seeing her in casual clothes. His eyes traced her figure all the way from her shoulders to her ankles and back up again.

She picked up a black clutch bag and looked inside it whilst mumbling to herself.

Something in Josh took over. He jumped out of his seat and firmly said, 'No!'

Joey's eyes widened in surprise. 'What?'

'What?'

'You just said no.'

I don't know what I'm saying.

'I… I thought you were going on your bike.'

She glanced down at her clothes.

He shook his head at himself. 'No, of course not. Not the best idea. Would you like me to give you a lift?'

She looked even more surprised if not confused. 'You want to drop me off to my date?'

Not really.

He gave a half-shrug and scrunched his toes into the pale-green rug beneath him.

A tooting sound came from outside.

Joey turned to the front door. 'That's my cab.'

Josh froze as she wrapped her dark coat around her and stepped outside into the porch light.

How can I stop this? How can I make her stay?

'Have fun,' he called out.

Have fun? Seriously!

He ran to the door before she had a chance to walk down the pathway. 'Jo, wait.'

She held her coat across her neck. It was dark outside and cold.

'Do you have enough money?' he asked.

What the hell did I just say? I sound like her dad.

A hint of a smirk hit her pink lips. 'I'm good, thanks.'

'Okay,' he mumbled to himself. 'Just watch him. He has tactics.'

Joey was looking less and less impressed by the second. 'Tactics?'

Josh tilted his head to one side. Words failed him.

She turned away and headed for the cab.

He had little choice. She was going on her date. His shoulders slumped lower than his heart. He made a grab for his phone.

'Hello, Rusty, I really need a drink.'

216

'Okay, Josh. Tell me what happened?'

Josh moved over towards the stairs and slumped down to the second step. 'Joey's just gone on a date with Wendall. He's local. She's known him years.' He sighed, resting one hand on his head. 'I just don't get it. I really thought I'd made a breakthrough with her, with us, but, obviously, that's a nope.'

'Are you sure it's a date?'

Josh rolled his weary eyes up to look over at the door. Her black lace underwear flashed through his mind. 'I'm sure.'

Rusty's breath rustled down the phone. 'I'm sorry, Josh. You tried, and that's what counts here, but we both know you can't make someone fall in love with you.'

His jaw tensed with frustration. 'But that's the thing. I thought she had fallen in love with me. I was so sure of it. You told me to remember her eyes, and they were filled with love towards me. I saw it. I know I saw it. Now I feel as though I'm going mad. That I'm seeing things. I just want to come back to New York.'

'No, you don't, Josh. If you really felt that way, you wouldn't have called me. You would have got on a plane by now.'

Josh stared at the door. He swallowed hard and rolled back tears. 'I'm not coping very well right now, Rusty.' His voice was cracked. He bit in his lip to stop it from trembling. 'I love her so much, but she doesn't want anything serious. She's just proven that tonight.' He took a deep breath. 'I don't want to be here anymore. I can't stay here and watch her see other men. I seriously cannot do that.'

The thought of Wendall seeing her in the underwear she had flaunted in front of him was making him feel sick.

'She even showed me the underwear she's wearing tonight. For him.'

'She did?'

Josh frowned, as he was sure he could hear a smile in Rusty's voice. 'Why did you say it like that?'

'Just sounds hopeful.'

Josh removed the phone from his ear for one second to glance at it with raised eyebrows. 'Hopeful? What, like for Wendall?'

Rusty breathed out a short laugh. 'No, Josh, for you. Think about it. Why would she show you what underwear she is wearing for her date with another man?'

He gave a half-shrug. 'That's how much of a best mate I am to her.'

'I'm picking up on something different.'

'All the way from New York?'

There was a lightness to Rusty's tone as he said, 'Yes, Josh, all the way from New York.'

Josh widened his eyes in amazement. 'Well, I'm listening.'

'Have you thought that she might have been trying to make you jealous?'

Josh lowered his eyebrows. 'Why would she do that? She's not that type of person. She's actually quite straightforward.'

'Did you do anything that might make her feel unwanted at all?'

He straightened his back. 'I can't think of anything. I can't really think much at all at the moment.'

'Josh, I know we've spoken about this at great length, but I really do think that now is the time, my friend. This has gone on long enough. You need to just tell her exactly how you feel.'

'But I had a plan. I was going to take things slowly. Win her heart. Not sleep with her.' He stopped talking and huffed.

'Why did I have to go and sleep with her? What's wrong with me? Why do I always mess up my life?'

'Listen to me, Josh. You haven't messed anything up. This is not a setback. It's another way of learning how to cope. So far, you're doing great.'

Josh wrinkled his nose. 'Hardly! I wanted a drink when I rang you.'

'Exactly. You didn't hit the bottle. You called me. Plus, you didn't run away. You're still there, right now, trying to figure out a way forward. Those are huge steps. You need to feel proud of yourself. I'm proud of you.'

Josh rubbed his palm over his knee. The change in the way he handled bad situations had been pointed out to him, and now he could see it too. 'I really have come a long way, haven't I?'

'Yes, Josh, you have. There are always going to be incredibly hard things we have to deal with in life, because that's life. As long as we learn that when one way doesn't help us, we can choose another, we'll be okay. We might not be tip top, but sometimes okay is good enough.'

Josh took a moment for Rusty's words to sink deep. 'I feel hurt. I'm definitely not tip top, but I am okay.'

'That's because you found another way, my friend.'

34

Joey

Swan Lake was the poshest restaurant in Sandly. It was decorated with a hint of 1930s style and had an incredibly magical view of a lit-up lake, which homed swans. The thick-cloth-covered tables inside were large and round, even the tables for two. The spaces in between were wide, giving each table a certain amount of privacy. Long dark drapes sat either side of floor-to-ceiling windows, and crystal chandeliers hung high above. A white grand piano took up the corner closest to the arched column entrance to the dining room. A tall man, wearing a tuxedo, tinkled away on the keys, filling the air with a soft, light sound.

Joey was sitting on an ornate, deep-green, velvet chair opposite Wendall. She had never felt so uncomfortable in her life. Swan Lake had never been her thing. She much preferred dinner at The Ugly Duckling, but she didn't want to ask Wendall to go there, as she wanted the opportunity to dress up for once just so she could show Josh that she could look good. She tried not to glance around the room like a tourist. Wendall looked comfortable in their surroundings, and she wanted to give off the same impression, even though she knew that he knew that she didn't hang out in posh places.

'You okay, Jo?' he asked. 'You seem a little lost.'

She avoided his eyes, turning hers to his dark-blue suit. 'I was just thinking what a nice suit you have there.'

Wendall glanced down at his jacket and beamed his shiny dental veneers. 'Thank you.' His cheery face looked over at her. 'It cost two grand.'

'Oh.' She wasn't quite sure what to say to that. 'Is that… good?'

His dark eyes narrowed as his brow furrowed. 'Yeah. You can buy a suit for thirty quid, you know. How much did your dress cost?'

'Erm, I didn't buy it. I borrowed it from Molly Hadley.'

Wendall gave a polite nod. 'You wear it well.'

It's a bit bloody clingy, and these stupid knickers keep going up my bum. I don't know what possessed me to buy them. I do know. I got them to show Josh one night. I guess I did show him. Not sure he even looked. Probably too busy thinking about the leggy blonde.

'This is a bit of a surprise, Jo. I really didn't think you'd ever talk to me again after what happened with Loretta.'

'I figured, if you treat me to a meal here, I'll let you off.'

Wendall laughed. 'Expensive treat, but okay.'

'I can pay half. I don't mind.'

He grinned into his red wine. 'I think I can manage, Jo-Jo.'

Jo-Jo?

'Besides, you only ordered mushroom linguine,' he added, glancing at her plate. 'Hardly breaking a sweat in my wallet.'

Joey smiled politely, as she really had no idea how to respond.

A waitress, dressed in black, pushed a silver-and-chrome trolley past their table. On it was a white saucer drizzled in yellow sauce with an orb of lemon sorbet on top. Another plate was in the shape of a crescent moon and had three white chocolate-infused balls nestled there. Another dish was on a black slate. Raspberry coulis was sprinkled over the base, and a thin-crust tart filled with rich dark chocolate sat to one edge. The last dessert was a slice of hot peach pie resting in place upon a dipped white bowl that had a nook filled by a small white jug holding steaming custard.

Joey's eyes widened. 'Wow, did you see that lot?'

'I would have thought you would be sick of seeing desserts, what with all the sweet fancies you make.'

'I love desserts. Best part of any meal.'

'Well, I can't argue with that. Which one caught your eye?'

She smiled widely. 'All of them.'

Wendall was saying something about not being able to buy all of them, but Joey stopped listening. Out of the top of her lashes she spotted Jake and Anna being guided to a table over the other side of the room.

Oh crap! I hope he doesn't see me.

It was too late. Anna had seen her. She was facing their way and frowning with confused amusement.

Wendall was cutting up steak, and Anna had pulled Jake back towards her direction when he went to look over his shoulder at what she had frowned at. She stood, saying something to Jake, and then walked towards the toilets, discreetly waving her hand at Joey to follow her.

'Won't be a minute, Wendall. I need the loo.'

'Okay,' he mumbled through his food.

Joey quickly made her way out of the dining room, avoiding Jake altogether. She took a breath as she entered the boutique-styled bathroom.

'What the hell are you doing in here with Wendall James?' Anna's voice sounded both inquisitive and annoyed.

Joey moved around her to stand over by the long ornate mirror at the end of the room. 'I'm on a date. Sort of.'

Anna's brow wrinkled. 'A date?'

'Sort of.'

'What does that mean? And more to the point, why?'

Joey flapped her arms up to her sides. 'I was bloody fuming, that's why. Last night, Josh... Well, we got close, and today, get this, today, he went out to lunch with some blonde leggy woman. God knows where he met her, but still, Anna. It bloody well hurt.'

'Are you talking about Regina?'

'Who?'

Anna was struggling to keep a straight face. 'Regina Patterson. She works for Café Diths. She's a board member. One of John's team. She was here today for a business meeting with Jake and Josh. They went to the Italian place over here, Bella's. Jake's friend owns the place. They call him Spiky Rick.'

'Yeah, I know who he is. Business meeting?'

Joey watched Anna's face fill with sympathy.

'You thought Josh was on a date with her?'

Joey blinked slowly and took a deep breath as nauseating embarrassment flooded through every part of her. 'Oh God, I didn't know. He hadn't contacted me all morning. I thought he had... Oh, never mind.'

Anna affectionally touched her arm. 'Jo, they were talking about selling your bespoke lollipops in their shops.'

Joey's mouth gaped. 'Their shops?'

Anna nodded slowly. 'Yes. You know, those shops that they have. The ones that are all over the world.'

Joey clutched her stomach. 'I feel sick.'

Anna pulled in her lips.

'Don't you laugh, Anna.'

Anna shook her head. Her cheeks were flushed and her lips were trembling. She couldn't hold it in any longer. 'I'm so sorry, Joey, but it's a little funny.'

Joey fought back a grin. 'It's not at all funny.'

'You're on a date with a man you're not interested in just because you thought Josh didn't care about you.'

Joey turned to the mirror and looked herself over. 'And I'm wearing one of Molly's dresses.'

'You look gorgeous, by the way.'

Joey took a deep breath. 'I do not want to be here, Anna.'

Anna looked at her through the mirror. 'Then go be where you want to be, Joey.'

* * *

The cab ride home seemed to take forever. Wendall was pretty forgiving about her early departure. He said goodbye to her at the taxi. He didn't try to kiss her and hoped she felt better soon.

The driver was taking his time because it had started to pour down.

Joey gloomily watched the raindrops bash the front window as the cab pulled up outside Honeybee Cottage. For a moment, she didn't want to get out and go inside to face Josh.

'Thanks, Ron,' she said, handing over some money.

She placed her coat over her head, for what good it did, as she made a quick dash for the gate.

The lock wouldn't unfasten, causing her to lower her other arm to tackle the small metal gadget. It still wouldn't budge.

Come on, stupid thing.

Her coat draped down to sit upon her shoulders. She was getting soaked.

That's it! I've had enough.

She quickly hitched up her dress to the top of her thighs and climbed over the fence. Her coat got caught on a wooden spike, tugging her backwards. She slipped in the slushy mud on the other side and landed on her back.

You have got to be kidding me!

She got up just as quickly as she fell. Her ankle buckled as her left foot hit the pathway, and the heel to her shoe snapped clean off. 'Whoa!' Her knees hit the ground. She swore under her breath and stumbled to a stand.

She limped her way into the house. Her muddy coat was draped over her bag in one hand, and the broken heel sat in her other.

Bobby Darin's "Dream Lover" was playing quietly in the living room.

She locked eyes with Josh's curious stare as she bypassed the room to sling her coat onto the hallway banister.

He removed his glasses and peered along his nose at her.

Joey was a wet, slumped, muddy mess. Her loose curls resembled rat tails, and her half-raised dress was clinging even more to her damp skin, revealing a graze on her right knee. Mascara was streaked down her cheeks, and a line of blood trailed her cut ankle. She waved her broken shoe at him, then quietly headed upstairs.

She fought vigorously to get out of her skin-tight dress. It was practically glued to her. She tugged and pulled till she was breathless and her shoulders ached.

Great! Bloody great. Death by dress. I'm actually going to be found dead this way. How did Joey Walker die? She was found slumped on her bedroom floor with part of her dress halfway up her stomach and the other part strangling her left breast. It was a pitiful end to her pitiful life.

She finally managed to whip it off over her head. She caught her breath and quickly lost her underwear as well.

She stood there for a moment, feeling cold, wet, muddy, bruised, and extremely sorry for herself.

She limped into the bathroom and walked straight into the sky-blue tiled shower. She slowly wiped a wet face cloth over her face and muddy arms, and then squirted a blob of Jake's shampoo on her head and washed away her disastrous evening.

After ten minutes of staring at the floor, she switched off the shower, stepped out, and gently patted herself dry. She removed her green flannel pyjama shirt from the hook on the back of the door and shrugged it over her head. She flopped to the floor, wondering why she hadn't got a plaster for her cut ankle first. The thin slice was stinging and still leaking blood.

She winced at the wound. 'Ouch!'

She leant up to pull open the oak drawer under the sink, but Josh's hand got there first. She slumped back down and sat quietly whilst he went about tending to her knee and ankle. She slid a towel off the side of the bath and rubbed the ends of her hair.

The silence in the bathroom wasn't awkward or intense or anything. It was just plain old silence.

When Josh seemed satisfied with his work, he helped her to stand, put her pyjama bottoms on, combed her hair, and then picked her up, draping her across his arms, and carried her downstairs to the sofa.

Joey smiled weakly as he placed a chunky green-and-cream blanket over her lap.

'Do you want some Horlicks?' he asked quietly.

Still feeling rather sorry for herself, she feebly nodded.

35

Josh

Josh smiled weakly over at his brother. 'Thanks for letting me know last night, Jake.'

Jake smiled back. He nodded towards the television. 'Watch the film.'

Josh looked up at the 55-inch TV on the wall above the fireplace. 'I can't concentrate.'

Jake turned away from the old John Wayne movie that they were only watching because John Wayne reminded them of their grandfather.

'I thought you came up to Starlight to help clear your head.'

That had been Josh's plan. 'I'm trying.'

'At least you now know Joey doesn't have a thing for Wendall James.'

'Is Anna talking to you yet?'

Jake looked over his shoulder before responding. 'Well, she wasn't happy that I called you as soon as she told me in the restaurant, but she's all right now.'

'I'm glad you called me, because I really wanted a drink.'

Jake looked worried. 'Josh…'

'I didn't,' he quickly said. 'I called Rusty instead.'

Jake took a deep breath. 'Well done.'

Max trotted over and climbed up on the sofa between the two men, looking sheepishly at Jake whilst snuggling into Josh's legs.

'You're not allowed on the furniture, Max,' said Jake.

Josh wriggled his fingers into Max's soft fur. 'He likes it up here. It's comfy.'

Jake stared wide-eyed down at Max's brown bed in front of the crackling fire. 'He has a perfectly comfortable bed right there, and well he knows it.'

Josh grinned at the dog.

Max avoided eye contact with Jake.

Jake looked at Josh. 'He only does this when you're here, you know.'

'He's my mate, aren't you, Max?'

Max burrowed his damp nose into Josh's blue jumper.

'At least someone loves me,' muttered Josh.

'We all love you, Josh, even Joey. You might know that if you spoke to her about it for once.'

Josh ignored him and faced the TV.

Anna approached the back of the sofa and leaned over to stroke Max. 'You're not supposed to be up here, Max.'

Jake held up his palms. 'I have already said that, but nobody listens to me.'

'Hmm,' mumbled Anna, glancing sideways at him.

Josh watched Jake's eyes hit level smouldering and wondered if Anna would fall for that look.

She walked around the sofa and curled down onto Jake's lap and smooshed her head into his shoulder.

Unbelievable. They are like putty in each other's hands.

Josh held back the desire to shake his head as Jake released a proud smile.

'So, Josh,' said Anna, after she had stopped smiling lovingly at Jake. 'Are you stopping for dinner?'

'No. Joey's making me a vegan pizza.'

Anna frowned. 'Vegan pizza. How does that work? Can you get vegan cheese?'

Josh nodded. 'Yep, and she's been acting weird all day. She didn't even go to the tea shop. I told her she didn't have to cook for me, but she practically bit my head off. So, whether I like it or not, I'm having vegan pizza for my dinner tonight.'

'She probably wants to make it up to you, that's all,' said Anna.

'She has no need to make anything up to me.'

Jake huffed. 'You know, your life would be a lot less complicated if you actually spoke to Joey. You two are starting to become a bloody nightmare.'

Anna scorned him.

Josh scrunched his nose. 'Just say what you really think, Jake.'

Jake pulled Anna closer to him, as she had leaned away. 'From an outsider's point of view, it's quite frustrating to watch.'

Anna looked sympathetic. 'He does have a point, Josh.'

'I came here to spend some time with Gramps,' said Josh, pointing at the TV, 'not to have you two tag-team me with your vast knowledge of love. Remind me, how long have you two been together now? Since November, isn't it?'

'Oh, be quiet,' said Jake.

'A short amount of time but filled with pure love,' said Anna, smiling at Jake.

Josh screwed his face up, as his brother looked ready to take Anna to bed.

'Right,' she said, getting up. 'I'm off for a bath. Jake is ordering Chinese food for our dinner tonight, so that's good. I don't have to cook.'

Jake reached forward to tickle her ribs. 'What a cheek. I always cook.'

Anna jolted away. 'It's not my fault your grandmother made both you boys exceptionally good chefs.'

Josh and Jake nodded in agreement.

'It's true,' said Josh.

Jake waited until she had gone upstairs. He leaned closer to Josh. 'I'm going to ask her to marry me.'

Something inside of Josh wasn't surprised. 'Oh, when?'

'Valentine's Day. I'm flying to London in a couple of days to buy her a ring.'

Josh smiled warmly. He was pleased his brother had found love. 'That's great, Jake. I'm really happy for you, but you're not doing this because of what we talked about, are you? You know, Scott Harper. Your insecurities.'

Jake frowned. 'No. Of course not. I've had this planned for ages. I wanted to marry her the first time we kissed.'

Josh raised his brow. 'I guess, when you know, you know.'

'Gramps knew the moment he saw Gran. It happens like that for some people.'

Josh thought about how long he had loved Joey.

Jake nudged him with his foot. 'Why don't you come to London with me. We can stay overnight. Go and see one of those musicals you like.'

Josh grinned. 'You like them too. I know you do.'

'What do you think. Do you want to come? I'd like you there.'

'Okay. I'll come. Maybe I'll buy Joey something too.'

Jake sat back. 'I think it's time, Josh. Tell her tonight. I was so relieved when I finally told Anna how I felt about her. Even if you get a knockback, you will still feel so much better for finally getting it off your chest. Trust me. Besides, I don't think she'll reject you. I think she's been waiting for you to say it first for a long time.'

* * *

Joey rinsed the plates under the tap and shook her head. 'That pizza wasn't bad. I am pleasantly surprised.'

Josh covered the glass salad bowl with clingfilm and put it in the fridge. He sat down at the round oak dining table that was near the door.

Joey glanced over her shoulder. 'Are you okay? You haven't spoken much today.'

That's it. I'm doing this. It's time.

'Come and sit down for a minute, will you, Jo. I want to talk to you about something.'

He could see the nerves in her eyes as she sat opposite him.

'What do you want to talk about?'

'I'm going to London in a couple of days with Jake…'

'And you're not coming back.'

What? No. That's not it.

'I'm coming back, Jo.' He paused. 'Do you want me to come back?'

'Yes.'

He was pleased she said it so quickly. 'Good. It's only for one night. Jake has something he wants to do, and he wants me to go with him.'

She looked slightly guarded as though she were bracing herself for bad news.

Josh twiddled his fingers on the table. 'Look, there's something I want to say, and I want to say it before I go. In fact, I've been wanting to say this for a long time.'

Too long.

She waited quietly.

He swallowed. 'I'm not sure how you're going to take this piece of information, but I'm done stressing over it.' He took a moment to steady his breathing. 'Jo, you're my first kiss. The one I lost my virginity to. You're the only woman I've said I love you to. I know that we love each other. We always have. You're my best friend, but I've been lying to you all this time.' He huffed to himself.

Come on, Josh. Just spit it out.

Joey's eyes had widened slightly. She looked apprehensive, but, unlike him, she sat still.

He could feel his brow tighten, so he tried to relax. 'What I want to say is… well, you have never been a beach romance to me. To me, you've always meant more than that.'

Stop rambling. Tell her straight.

He placed his hands down flat on the table and rolled his eyes up to meet hers. 'I love you, Joey Walker. I always have, and I always will, and not in a friend way. I'm in love with you. I've always been in love with you.' He couldn't hold her gaze any longer. His hands clasped tightly back together again. 'I don't want to hide that anymore. If it's just sex and a bit of fun for you, that's fine. I get it. Each to their own, but I want you to know that I have never had sex with you. Right back from our first time, and we both know what a disaster that was, I have only ever made love to you.' He looked at her again. 'I love you, Joey. I, honest to God, deep down within my heart of hearts, love you.'

36

Joey

His bright eyes looked underwater as tears blurred her vision. Ever since she was a young girl, she had longed to hear Josh Reynolds tell her that he was in love with her. Now he was sitting in their kitchen in their own cottage in Pepper Bay saying exactly that. Even the butterflies in her stomach were too overwhelmed to flutter. She couldn't move. She was just staring at him, lost for words. Not once, in all her daydreaming, did she think about what she would say in return. The standard response didn't seem big enough. She believed there was more she could say, but nothing was coming to her.

'Say something, Jo.'

He wasn't looking at her. He was embarrassed. Submissive. Scared. She couldn't work it out.

His voice was cracking under the pressure in the room. 'I would like to know how you feel.'

Everything, Josh.

'I…' Words lodged in her throat. She swallowed hard. 'Josh, I.'

He looked up. 'I only want the truth, Jo. Don't stroke my ego.'

Tears rolled down her cheeks.

He quickly got up and moved to the chair next to her. 'Hey, don't cry.' He wiped her tears.

Joey flung her arms around his neck and held on tightly. She knew her words were incoherent, as she couldn't hear them either due to her mouth pressed firmly into his jumper.

He didn't pull away. He just held her whilst she sobbed and mumbled.

Pull yourself together, Jo. Come on. This is what you've been dreaming of. Don't be a wreck.

She lifted her face and pulled a tissue from her cardigan pocket.

He smiled softly at her as she cleaned her face.

'Sorry about that,' she whispered.

'It's okay. As long as you're okay.'

She gave a slight nod and sniffed.

He placed his hand on her chin, lifting her face. 'We don't have to talk about this. I don't want to upset you.'

'You haven't.' She cleared her throat, as her words had sounded hoarse. She waved her hand in front of her face and smiled. 'I'm a bit of a mess.' Her laugh was as weak as her legs. She was glad she was sitting down.

He tucked her hair behind her ears and went to lean back.

She grabbed his warm hands. 'Josh, I've waited forever to hear you say what you just said. I always thought you looked at me as your holiday fling. A sure thing.' She huffed out a short laugh. 'It broke my heart every time you left.' Another tear fell from her eye. 'I love you so much. I...'

His mouth pressed against hers.

She tried to wipe her damp cheek with the tissue, but his hand reached up and held hers still. She stayed motionless on his lips. Not wanting to move a single muscle.

Josh slowly pulled away, scrunched his eyes tightly, and lowered his head. 'I can't believe we've wasted all this time.'

Joey rested her mouth on his hair. 'We haven't wasted any time. Not really. We still shared our time together. We still loved each other, even if we didn't say that we did.'

'Yeah, but we were both hurting.'

She kissed his head. 'I'm not hurting anymore, Josh.'

He slowly lifted his head. His eyes were glossed over, and his face slightly hot. 'I don't know how to feel, Jo. There are all these emotions running through me. I'm relieved I told you. Ecstatic you feel the same way. Deflated because of the past. It's just whirling inside of my head.'

Oh God, this man. He's so perfect. I love everything about him, and he loves me. He loves me.

She stroked his face and tenderly kissed his mouth. 'We're home now, Josh. We made it. We're together. The only emotion we need to focus on is our love.'

'I have so much love for you, Jo.'

She smiled warmly. 'Do you remember when we were teenagers and you told me that you would always come back to me?'

He rolled his eyes down. 'I broke that promise.'

'You didn't. You may have skipped some years, but you always came back.'

He looked at her. 'You always waited for me.'

Her eyes smiled his way. 'I did.'

The lines on his brow tightened. 'I promise you that I'll always come home to you. You are my home, Jo, and I'll never break that promise again.'

She kissed him. 'I don't want you to beat yourself up over it. I just want you to make love to me. Make love to me, Josh, and never stop.'

He smiled warmly and nudged her nose with his own. 'I can do that.'

She quickly swiped away another falling tear.

He stroked his thumb over her cheek. 'But you have to stop crying.'

Joey's laugh lines filled her face. 'I don't know where they're coming from.' Another tear fell. She raised her palm. 'See. I have no control.'

He leaned closer and kissed her teardrop, then slowly stood and took her hand.

'Where are we going?' she asked quietly, wiping away two more tears.

'Where do you want to go?'

'I don't care, as long as I'm with you. Oh God, that sounds so corny.'

He smiled his sexy smile. The one that made her cave every time. 'I liked it.'

'The bed would be comfortable.'

His azure eyes were suddenly full of authority. They locked into hers, and Joey felt her heart thump. This wasn't slow and sensual Josh looking at her now. This was heated and passionate Josh. Sensual Josh she could just about cope with. His slow and steady movements almost hypnotised her. Passionate Josh was a whole different experience altogether. She submitted to him. Weakened at just the shift in his bright eyes.

She followed him to her bedroom. Her heart was pounding, ready and waiting for the moment he turned and unleashed his heat.

His hand slipped from hers.

She slowly closed the door whilst facing his back. She knew how the night was going to play out. This wasn't their first time in this mood.

Josh was standing still. 'Take your clothes off.' His firm tone caused her to quietly gasp.

She scrambled out of her cardigan and started to unbutton her shirt as warmth churned in her stomach.

He turned and watched her.

Her heart skipped a beat. Her fingers were fumbling over the buttons. She bit in her lip awkwardly, as her attempt to seductively remove her shirt wasn't going to plan, thanks to a piece of cotton entangled around one button.

Josh propelled himself towards her. Slamming her back into the door. His hands pinned her arms high above her head.

Joey gasped. She started panting as his mouth hit her neck.

He reached down and grabbed her shirt and ripped it open, causing small white buttons to fly across the room.

She frowned. 'Josh, I really liked that shirt.'

He stopped caressing her neck and lifted his head to look blankly at her. 'Are you going to stay in character, or what?'

'Oh, yeah, sorry.' She rested her head back against the door and closed her eyes.

'Jo?'

'Hmm?'

'Did I just hurt your back?'

She brought her head forward. 'Josh, my back is fine. You know I'll tell you if you're hurting me.'

He gave a slight head shake to his right. 'Yeah, I know, but I thought it was a bit rough. I didn't know there was that much of a gap between you and the door.'

'It's fine. I'm fine. Carry on.'

He pressed his lips down heavily onto hers.

Joey mumbled through their locked mouths. 'Do you think we should have a safe word?' She could feel his lips twist into a smirk.

He pulled his mouth away. 'Why do we need a safe word?'

She gave a slight shrug. 'It's a thing. Isn't it?'

His smile had widened. 'Yeah, but not for us. We don't go that far.'

She wrinkled her nose. 'It was just an idea.'

He sighed. 'If you want a safe word, we'll use a safe word.'

Joey kissed him and then pulled back, narrowing her eyes. 'What word should we use?'

Josh kissed her neck. 'Whatever word you want.'

'I don't think we need one.' She paused for thought. 'Might be fun though.'

He looked up in amusement. 'Red. Shout red. Okay?'

She giggled. 'I think I might laugh if I say that.'

'Then choose something else.'

'I think I might laugh at whatever we choose.'

He raised his eyebrows. 'Oh, I know you'll laugh.'

She gave a slight shake of the head. 'We don't need one.'

He agreed. 'No, we don't.'

'Okay, I'm ready now.'

He looked at her to doublecheck. He was half smiling and half serious. 'Are you sure?'

Her perfect teeth beamed his way.

He placed his mouth back on her neck, but his kisses had slowed.

Joey sighed. 'Josh, what's wrong now?'

He took a step back. 'I don't know. What with you and the shirt, and then the door, and then the safe word, I feel off my game now.'

She slumped inside at the fact the authority in his eyes had disappeared. It was one of her favourite looks, and she wanted it back. She quickly removed all of her clothes and stood there naked, awkwardly leaning one arm up against the door.

Josh raised his brow and corners of his mouth.

She tried to mimic his steamy, sexy act. She pointed a finger at him. 'Take your clothes off.'

His eyes were filled with amusement as he pulled in his lips and stripped.

She softened her face and voice. 'Oh, Josh. You look like you're from a sexy aftershave advert.'

Josh looked perplexed. 'I don't think they're naked in those.'

She smiled warmly and wiggled her finger at him. 'Come here.'

He closed in on her until their faces were inches apart.

She softly kissed his lips and circled his nose with her own, then she pulled away.

'You know what to do, Josh,' she said, using her best husky voice.

He blinked and intensity filled his eyes.

Joey was pressed against the door. She lifted her legs and wrapped them around him. She could feel the heat from his mouth over her collarbone.

He pulled away, and she met his lips, kissing him passionately, wanting him, needing him. He turned and walked across the room to drop her down onto the bed.

She gasped with delight as she hit the mattress, slowly rolling her eyes up to meet the fire in his gaze. She dipped her head submissively as he stepped towards her.

He reached down and slowly twirled the back of her hair around his hand. His movement so soft, so gentle. Then, with one tug, he raised her face so that she was forced to look up at him. 'What do we say?' he demanded.

'Yes.'

'Yes, please.'

'Yes, please.'

His jaw tightened. 'Please, sir.'

She slapped the side of his thigh.

Josh grinned mischievously. 'Oh come on. Just say it one time.'

Joey held off her smile, blinked slowly, moistened her lips with her tongue, and in her best sexy voice she quietly said, 'Please, sir.'

Josh lost all trace of humour in his smile as he swallowed hard.

She lightly stroked her fingertips across the back of his knee. 'Josh. I'm ready.'

His eyes darkened once more as she softly kissed his hip.

37

Josh

Whenever John Reynolds wanted to buy jewellery, he always went to see his old friend Archie Halls in a small shop in Hatton Garden. Archie had learnt the craft from his own father and had passed his expertise down to his son, Walter. Their business was called A H of London. It had expanded from a corner shop to three shops in length once Archie's fingers were too old to work and Walter had taken over the business.

Josh and Jake sat at Archie's old dark-wood desk in the back room of the original part of the shop.

Walter Halls had closed off that section, giving his customers his very best VIP treatment.

Champagne had been offered but tea asked for instead. A small tray of bespoke biscuits joined the silver tea set that sat just to the side of the desk.

A purple velvet ring tray was in front of Jake. An array of diamond rings sparkled up at him.

Josh stroked his finger over the black velvet cloth that was laid out on the desk in front of him. 'There's a lot of choice, Walt.'

Walter held one of the rings between two fingers. 'There are many cuts, carats, and metals. I have brought a variety, so you get an idea. It can be overwhelming shopping for an engagement ring.'

Jake nodded his agreement. 'Especially when you're not entirely sure what she would want.' He narrowed his eyes at the shiny diamonds gleaming his way.

Walter had his own shine about him, from his bald head to the twinkle in his beady blue eyes. He smiled, revealing perfect white teeth. 'This is why I am here. So, let's start with some questions that you might find helpful.'

Josh watched his brother studying the rings with such seriousness. He already knew which one he would pick if he were buying for Joey and those were his only choice.

Walter placed down the ring he was holding so that it sat upon the black cloth. 'What kind of jewellery does she wear often?'

Jake's eyes rolled up from the tray. 'She's not really a jewellery person.'

Walter's pale face was animated as he absorbed the information. 'Okay. What are her hands like?'

Josh thought about Joey's long slender fingers.

'Erm, small, dainty, not too slim, but not fat.'

Josh couldn't be bothered to fight back the growing grin on his face. 'So, medium-size then?'

Jake looked over at him. 'I guess.'

'Do you have a picture of her?' asked Walter.

Jake seemed pleased. His stern expression softened. 'Sure.' He pulled out his phone and tapped at the screen. He proudly offered it to Walter. 'That's Anna.'

Walter removed his fine-rimmed glasses and studied the photo. 'Hmm.'

Jake frowned, making Josh laugh inside.

'What does hmm mean?'

'I'm getting a feel for her character through her face,' said Walter.

Josh was just as impressed as Jake. 'You can do that?'

Walter grinned. 'It's one of my talents.'

Josh laughed. 'That is a good talent to have. So, what's your verdict?'

Jake frowned with annoyance at him.

Walter was still staring at the screen. 'Homely girl. Kind. Low maintenance.'

'I'm not sure I like that term,' said Jake.

Josh nudged him. 'He's right though.' He looked at Walter. 'She's very sweet, but don't be fooled. She can put Jake back in his place when she wants to. She doesn't even have to say anything either. She just shows him her eyes and he melts.'

'I do not melt.'

Josh winked at Walter. 'He totally melts.'

Walter handed back the phone. He glanced down at the expensive collection on the desk. His hand hovered over the rings, and then he selected a thin gold band with a small princess cut. 'Delicate, understated, ideal for someone who doesn't wear much jewellery.'

Jake and Josh looked down at the ring.

'It's cute,' said Josh.

Jake turned to him with a look that was asking for help.

Josh nodded at the ring. 'I think that's the one. I think that would suit Anna. I also think she won't care which one you pick.'

Walter leaned back and smiled. 'Ah, true love.'

Josh grinned at him. 'Aren't all your engagement ring customers loved-up?'

Walter wrinkled his nose. 'I'm not so sure. Sometimes there are arguments.'

Josh was surprised. 'Really?'

Walter raised his palms. 'When the lady is here choosing for herself, love doesn't always shine through.'

Josh laughed. He glanced at Jake, but Jake was too busy agonising over the ring to join in the conversation.

Walter allowed Jake the time he needed. He turned his attention to Josh. 'So, Josh, what about you? Who is your young lady?'

Josh smiled warmly. Just the thought of Joey brought sunshine to his soul. 'Her name is Joey Walker, and she's a baker.' He looked down at his black bag on the floor. 'She also makes bespoke lollipops.' He pulled one out of his bag and handed it over.

Walter held it up to the light. 'What is that inside, a dandelion?'

Josh pointed over at the small clear circle. 'You can eat them, and she's going to be making more soon using different edible flowers.'

Walter smiled and placed it down on the desk. 'Send me some more, Josh. They will make nice gifts to add to my tea set.'

'Thank you. I will.'

Walter gently tapped the sweet. 'I'll be eating this one myself.'

Josh looked over at the biscuits. 'Will it be okay if I take one of those lavender biscuits with me. I want to show Joey.'

Walter raised one hand. 'I'll have some sent to your address first thing in the morning.'

'Thanks, Walt.'

'So, are you ready to propose to Joey Walker yet?' he asked.

Josh knew there was no other woman in the world that he wanted to spend the rest of his life with. 'Yes, but these rings aren't for her.'

Walter's eyes were filled with delight and curiosity. 'Oh, I'm intrigued now. What would the delightful Joey prefer?'

'Her birthstone is Sapphire.'

'Ah, so that's who the eternity ring was for.' Walter nodded to himself. 'Carl told me about that. I was on holiday with friends when you were last here. It did raise questions that I wished Carl had asked. You know I would have asked.'

'I'll take it,' said Jake.

Walter picked up the phone on his desk. 'Bring me the sapphire ring collection. No, not that one. I want the one Leo just finished. Thank you.' He turned to Jake. 'Do you know her ring size?'

Jake looked baffled. He displayed his fingers like a starfish and glanced down at them.

Walter waved his hand at him. 'Show me some more photos. Don't worry. I have a knack for this too.'

The door opened behind them, and a young lady in a white blouse and black trousers placed a small tray in front of Josh.

'Yes, very good,' said Walter, giving her the cue to leave.

Josh looked at the four sapphire rings placed an inch apart on silky white material. The corners of his mouth curled.

So did Walter's. 'Ah, you know straight away, don't you, Josh?'

38

Joey

'Joey, what is that cake you're decorating?' asked Anna, peering over her shoulder.

Joey pointed over towards the other side of the shop's kitchen. 'Turn that radio down, please, Anna.'

Anna switched the small cream radio down low.

'I don't know why Ruby has it so loud. I think she's going deaf.'

'I heard that,' called out Ruby from the shop.

Joey turned back to the blue-and-white box-shaped cake she was adding straw-coloured fondant swirls to. 'It's a proposal cake. It's for Valentine's Day. The customer is going to put the ring box inside this, so I'm just finishing the padding, and then I've got a lid to make. It will rest upwards, like it has been opened. I have been asked to put rings inside cakes before, but I tell them it's dangerous. I don't want anyone choking. This way is safer. No one will choke on a ring box.'

Anna laughed. 'I've never heard of a proposal cake before.'

'You get all sorts nowadays,' said Joey, glancing at her opened notepad that held the pencil-drawn design. 'I've made a divorce cake before. It had blood dripping down the side and a groom lying at the bottom with a knife in his back. That was for Sharon. She's a bit extreme at times.'

Anna sat down on a stall and sipped her tea.

Ruby called out from the shopfront. 'I'll be right back. My Freddy's over the road. I just want a quick word with him.'

'Okay,' called back Joey. She heard Ruby mumble something as she was leaving. 'What's that, Rubes?'

'Scott's here.'

Anna poked her head out of the kitchen. 'Hello, Scott. You come for a green tea?'

Scott loosened the brown scarf around his neck. 'Yes, but I can wait.'

Joey called out to him. 'You can make it, if you want, Scott.'

He sat down at the table nearest the counter and kept his eyes on his lap. 'Thank you. I'll wait.'

Anna turned around to face Joey. 'He is so Clark Kent,' she mouthed.

Joey grinned to herself. 'How are you getting on working with Anna?' she called out to Scott.

Anna rolled her eyes.

'Very well, thank you,' said Scott softly.

Joey smiled at Anna.

Anna picked up her cup and sipped her tea whilst grinning at Joey's happy face. 'Ruby said you've not stopped smiling today.'

Joey glanced at her. 'What?'

'We know why. It's because Josh is back today.'

Joey's smile widened as far as it could go. 'He called an hour ago. Said they're leaving in a bit.'

'Yeah, I know. Jake called too. Frank's bringing them in his helicopter.'

'You've been in that, haven't you?'

Anna touched her heart. 'Oh my goodness, yes. That's how Jake brought me and Max to Pepper Bay. I didn't know whether to laugh or cry at the time. I was both scared and excited. It was very surreal.'

Joey laughed. 'I can just imagine Max in a helicopter. Sorry I can't let him in the shop while I'm working.'

'That's okay. He's happy with Robyn over the pub.'

The phone on the table in front of Joey started to vibrate.

Anna smiled warmly. 'I bet that's Josh.'

Joey frowned at the screen. 'It's Gran, and she's calling from her mobile. She never uses it. Reckons she doesn't know how to. Funny that. More like when it suits her. Hello, Gran. Everything all right?'

Josephine sounded breathless as she rambled into the phone. 'Tell him, Joey. Stop him. He can't, he can't. I've seen it. He's hurt. Falling, just falling…'

'Whoa! Slow down, Gran. I can't understand what you're saying. What's wrong? Who is hurt? Is it Nate?'

Anna locked eyes with Joey's concerned face. 'What's wrong?' she mouthed.

Joey jumped out of her chair, rushing towards the front of the shop. She could see Ruby outside talking to Freddy.

'Josh. It's Josh,' said Josephine. 'Not in the sky. He can't be up there.'

'Gran, you're not making any sense…'

'Call him, Joey, quickly. He mustn't. He just mustn't get into that helicopter. He's hurt. He can't breathe…'

'What? He's fine. I've not long spoken to him. He'll be here in a minute. Gran?'

Anna and Scott followed her out the shop.

Ruby and Freddy looked over at them, then followed Joey's eyes up towards the sky above the sea.

'What's wrong, love?' asked Ruby.

Frank's helicopter was in sight, just heading towards Pepper Bay.

'I can see him now, Gran,' said Joey. She turned to Anna. 'She's freaking out. Telling me to tell Josh not to get in the helicopter.'

Anna's worried eyes turned back to the sky.

'Give me that phone,' snapped Ruby, snatching it away. 'Now, you listen here, Josephine Walker. Joey doesn't need to hear any of your predictions. You're scaring everyone, as usual. Those Reynolds boys are fine. We can see them now...'

Freddy's words cut in, 'Is that smoke?' He pointed up at the approaching helicopter.

Anna gasped, slapping her hand to her mouth.

Joey took an unsteady step towards the beach.

Before anyone could say another word, the helicopter fell from the sky.

Anna's scream was muffled by her hand, but Joey's voice was loud.

'Josh!'

Everyone ran down to the shingles, but Joey didn't stop. She entered the sea and went straight into a front crawl, pushing against the icy waves. Her body stopped moving. She was being dragged backwards. She turned to see Freddy holding her. He pulled her out of the sea and onto the shore where they collapsed down upon the small stones.

Joey screamed at him to let her go, but Freddy held on tightly.

'Look,' cried out Ruby, pointing out to sea.

Wes Morland's boat quickly came around the bay.

'My dad's there, Jo,' said Freddy. 'He'll help.'

'There's Frank,' said Anna.

They watched a man swimming away from the sinking aircraft. Wes grabbed him and helped get him in the boat. All eyes turned back to where the helicopter had plummeted.

Silence loomed and time stood still. Joey had no air in her lungs, and Anna was being held up by Ruby.

Joey jumped out of Freddy's hold as his arms loosened. 'There's Jake.'

Anna ran towards the shoreline. 'He's got Josh.'

Freddy made sure he still had a grip on Joey in case she headed into the sea again.

Jake's head was above water. He had Josh resting on his chest whilst he swam backwards like a lifeguard.

Freddy looked over his shoulder. 'Mum, Ren's on the boat. Call him. Find out how they are.'

Ruby quickly did as she was told. 'Ren, it's Ruby. We're watching from the beach.'

All eyes were forward but all ears were with Ruby.

Wes was pulling Josh out of Jake's arms.

Everyone watched Jake enter the boat and then disappear out of sight. The boat took off towards Sandly.

Ruby gasped. 'Oh my God!'

Everyone turned to her glossy eyes.

'I'll tell them.' She lowered the phone.

'What is it, Mum?'

'Josh isn't breathing.'

A whoosh of air left Joey's mouth with such force she doubled over, clutching her stomach.

Freddy held on to her.

'They've called an ambulance. You need to go straight to the hospital.'

Anna fumbled with her pocket. 'I have Jake's car in the car park. We can use that.'

Ruby nodded towards the shop. 'Quickly, Anna. Get Joey upstairs and into some dry clothes.'

Anna took Joey's hand.

251

Ruby turned to her son. 'I'll take care of the shops with Scott. You drive, Fred. Anna's in no state to be behind the wheel.' She gave him Joey's phone, and Anna handed over the car keys.

Joey couldn't see where she was being led. Tears blurred her vision. Anna was holding her hand, and Freddy was talking in her ear, but nothing made any sense. She didn't even know how her legs were moving, as she could no longer feel them.

* * *

The A&E was pretty quiet. A young lad was sitting in a wheelchair, with his leg in pain from a football accident. An older man was sitting in the far corner, coughing and sneezing, and two middle-aged women were quietly chatting to each other over by the main desk.

Joey, Anna, and Freddy were huddled together on hard, plastic, green chairs. They had been waiting ages for news, but no one had told them anything. Anna's eyes were sore, Freddy's face was drained of all colour, and Joey was being held together by shock alone.

One of the doctors arrived. A nurse whispered in his ear and nodded towards Freddy, who was watching.

'The doctor's here,' he said, waking the women out of their trance-like state.

'I understand you are the family of the people involved in the helicopter crash,' said the doctor.

'Yes,' replied Freddy. 'What's happening? We haven't had one update, and we've been here ages, and can you please tell us in words that we'll understand.'

'Of course,' said the doctor, looking sympathetic. 'I have some news now. The pilot is okay. He took a blow to the head and has had stitches. We've done the necessary scans, and we're happy to report that he will be fine. Quite the miracle man. Now, I understand one of the brothers is called Jake?'

Anna's eyes widened.

'Yes,' said Freddy. 'Jake Reynolds. He's the slightly older-looking one. We saw him dragging his brother into the boat.'

The doctor gave a slight nod. 'He has two cracked ribs and a broken ankle. We couldn't set his ankle because there were complications, so he has been taken for surgery. He has had a full body scan and a head scan. There is no internal bleeding. Once his ankle is repaired, he will be fine. His recovery will take a while, but he will be okay.'

'And Josh?' asked Freddy.

The one second hesitation that came from the doctor caused Joey to gasp for air.

'Josh was resuscitated by his brother on the boat. Jake saved his life.'

'Oh, thank God,' said Freddy.

'He's not out of the woods, I'm afraid,' said the doctor. 'He's still unconscious, but stable. He has cracked ribs, a broken leg, and swelling on his head. Now, I say on his head. It's not inside his head. It's a bad knock to his skull. He has no internal bleeding.'

'Will he be all right though?' asked Freddy.

'We hope so. We've done everything we can to make him comfortable. We're just waiting for him to wake up.'

'But he will wake up?' asked Freddy.

The doctor gave a slight nod. 'We're optimistic, but you have to know that these things can take time. His body is resting now, helping him to heal.' He added a warm smile.

'He's going to have quite a headache when he wakes up. We're monitoring him closely. Please, try not to worry.'

A porter standing in the main entrance called over to the doctor. 'Doc, what do you want me to do about the reporters out here? They want to know if they can come in.'

The doctor raised one hand. 'No, they can't. Call security, and have them on all doors.' He turned back to the bleak faces looking up at him. 'Come with me. I'll take you to a waiting room where you'll be more comfortable.'

Anna stood first. 'Can't we see them?'

'Soon,' said the doctor.

* * *

The small waiting room had bench seating that was soft and padded with pale-blue material. A water cooler sat in one corner, and a fake plant in another. A picture of ducks waddling through mud was on the wall near the water, and the room smelled like furniture polish. There weren't any windows, and there was just one door.

Nate and Tessie walked in, and Nate immediately sat next to Joey, who flung her arms around him tightly and burst out crying.

Tessie put her arm around Anna. 'Any more news?'

Anna shook her weary head.

Freddy stood up. 'Anna's given me a list of things to bring back here for Jake and Josh, so now you're here, I'll go and get on with that.'

Tessie smiled weakly towards him as he left the room.

'It's been ages,' said Anna. 'The doctor did say that once Jake comes out of his operation, he'll be in recovery for a while.'

Joey slowed her breathing as Nate dried her eyes. She had no energy left in her. Her head flopped onto his shoulder and stayed there.

Tessie rubbed Anna's hand. 'Those Reynolds are as tough as old boots. They're going to be just fine. I'll pop outside and see if I can get an update from someone.'

Nate nodded over at her, then waved Anna towards him so that he could hold her too.

39

Josh

'Don't over-knead the dough, Josh,' said Edith. 'That's fine how it is now. Put it in the bowl. Well done. Looks good, doesn't it? Now, cover it with that tea towel there, and we'll come back to that later. Your grandfather is going to love some of that bread with some stew tonight. Do you want me to make you a vegetable stew now that you are a vegan?'

'Yes, please, Gran, but how did you know that I no longer eat meat?'

'I know everything, Josh. I like to check on you every now and then, when you need me.'

'I always need you.'

'No, you don't. You're coping very well. I'm proud of you, and your brother. You can go see him now.'

'I don't want to. I want to stay with you. We're going to have stew.'

'You can still have stew. I'll make it just how you like it, and I'll send it to you.'

'Why can't I stay and have it here with you and Gramps?'

'Because you're needed elsewhere.'

'Please don't make me leave, Gran. I don't want to leave you.'

'I love you, Josh. I'll always be here when you need me. You don't have to worry about us leaving each other. I have never left you. Now, hurry along. Jake's waiting, and you know what he can be like. Tell Josephine I said hello.'

'Yes, Gran.'

'And give that baby a kiss from me.'

'What baby?'

* * *

*Why can't I see? It's so dark. Where am I? I'm not moving.
What's happened to my body? I can't move. My head hurts.
Jake? I can hear you. Jake. Can you hear me?*

'Oh God, Jake. You just fell out of the sky. I couldn't breathe,' said Anna.

'It's okay, Anna. I'm safe,' said Jake.

*Anna, don't cry. He's safe. I can hear him. Can't you hear
him, Anna? I can hear you both. Can you hear each other?*

'I lost the ring,' said Jake.

*Where's the ring? Oh, it's at the bottom of the sea. I told
you to have it sent to Pepper Bay. Never mind. It's not a big
deal.*

Anna huffed. 'I don't care about the ring. I don't need a ring, Jake. I just need you.'

'I'll buy you another one.'

'Let's just get married and forget about an engagement.'

'Is that what you want?'

'I love you so much, Jake Reynolds. I don't need rings or wedding days, just a marriage to you.'

'We can go to the registry office in Sandly.'

'As soon as Josh wakes up, we'll go.'

*I'm awake now. I'm right here. Can't you see me? We can
go right now. I'm here. I'm with you. Where are you? Why
can't I see you?*

'You know the nurse will tell me off for being on your bed,' said Anna.

'I don't care about their rules. I'm not letting you go. Don't cry, Anna. Rest now. I'm coming home tomorrow.'

Don't leave without me, Jake. Please don't leave me. It's dark. I need you. Jake, I'm scared. Something feels wrong. Where are you? Don't leave me. You promised you'd always be there for me. I feel dizzy. What's happening to me? Did I drink last night? Where's Jake? I thought I just heard him. Someone's holding my hand. Who's touching me?

* * *

Misty white clouds held back a bright light that was fighting its way through. Josh stood there watching the struggle before him. Muffled voices seemed to whizz past, causing his head to jolt. He tried to catch the words but some of them were too fast. He closed his eyes and strained his ears.

A faint sound of a siren came and went. He squirmed away from hands grabbing him.

The smell filling the air was the same smell he remembered from when his parents had died. The tall man with the deep voice smelled like that. The blue gown he was wearing smelled like that. The cold room with the magnolia walls smelled like that. Stale, lingering disinfectant.

'Josh, can you hear me?'

Who are you? Why are you touching me?

'His blood pressure's stabilising.'

Who are you talking about? Whose blood pressure? Are you with my mum? Is it my dad? Can you save them? Please save them. Save my parents. I don't want them to die. I don't know what to do. Help me. Help them. Somebody, do something.

The white clouds dispersed and the light blinded him even with his eyes closed. The feeling of high altitude hit him.

Oh, take me down. I'm too high. I feel sick. My head hurts. I can't breathe properly. Where's my pulse? I can't feel my

heart. I have a heart. Where's my heart? Did you take it?
Why would you take it? Why would you do this to me? I don't
like it here. Please, let me go. Please.

* * *

Joey was sitting on a bale of straw in her father's barn. The
air was warm and filled with the faint smell of manure. She
was seventeen, with a fresh complexion and long golden
hair. Straw was stuck on her green dress. The dress that Josh
could feel himself touching. The material was soft and thin.

He leaned over and kissed her cheek and smiled warmly
at her.

'You're leaving tomorrow,' she said quietly.

'School starts back soon.'

'For you. I'll be working in your Gran's tea shop.'

'You like it there.'

'I do, but I like it here with you too.'

'Jo, what we just did. Well, I can do better.'

She giggled. 'We both can, and we will, next time, when
you come back next year for the summer. You will come
back, won't you?'

'Yeah.'

'You can't practice with anyone else, Josh.'

'I won't.' He felt the warm skin of her cheek beneath his
lips.

'I'll wait for you,' she whispered close to his ear.

'I'll come back.'

'You have to promise, Josh.'

'I promise.'

He felt straw behind his head as she pushed him down to
the bale. Taupe eyes were gazing into his. A wide, perfect
smile beamed towards his mouth.

'I'll always wait for you, Josh Reynolds.'
'I'll always come back to you, Joey Walker.'

* * *

Josh could see green grass all around him. The air was mild and the long blades were cool. The sun was setting, creating a warm glow above him. His head was resting on his hands, and his body felt tired slumped there on the ground.

Joey leaned up on her elbow and grinned at him.

He tried not to laugh at the mischievous look in her eyes. 'I think we're getting too old to fool around in the grass, Jo.'

'Nonsense. We're going to do this when we're in our eighties.'

Josh breathed out a laugh. 'Is that a date?'

'Yes. Make a note. Meet me up at Sandly View in, what shall we say? Sixty years from today.'

'I don't think I want to wait that long.'

'You won't have to. You just have to come back every year.'

'I always come back.'

'You didn't last year.'

'I'm sorry, Jo.'

'We're older now. I guess we both have other things to do.'

Josh felt her lips on his. He closed his eyes and silently asked whoever was listening to his thoughts to make sure he always found a way back to Joey Walker.

* * *

'Please wake up, Josh. I need you,' whispered Joey.
I'm here, Jo. Where are you?

'There should be some change by now,' said Jake, sounding annoyed.

'Jake, can't you bring over better doctors or something?' A nervous rattle filled her voice.

'He's fine, Jo. You heard what they said. He'll wake up soon.'

I'm awake now, Jake. Why don't you know that? Why do people keep ignoring me? Move, Josh. Bloody move. Show them you're awake. Ha! That was my finger. I felt it. It moved.

'Did you see that, Jake?'

'What? What was it?'

'His finger moved. I saw it. It moved. His index finger. It just twitched.'

'The nurse did say that can happen.'

'Go and tell her.'

Yes, go and tell someone. I'm starting to get annoyed. Let me see if I can do it again. Okay, finger, move. Move. Come on. You just moved a second ago. Move. Argh! Move.

'Did he tell you? Josh's finger moved.'

'I'm afraid there's no change.'

'What do you mean there's no change. Check the machine again. I'm telling you he moved,' said Joey.

'It's all right, Jo. Settle down,' said Jake.

'She doesn't know what she's talking about.'

You tell him, Jo. Tell them all. Jo, why aren't you talking? Where are you? Joey? Where has she gone now? Jo. Jo.

* * *

'Gran? Oh, Gran, am I glad to see you. You told me to leave, but I can't move. I can't go anywhere, and I really tried.'

'Have you made your decision yet, Josh?'

'What decision, Gran?'

'Where you're having your dinner tonight.'

'I want to have dinner with you.'

'Follow me, then.'

'But what about Joey. Can she come too?'

'No, Josh. Just you.'

'If I go with you, will I see her again?'

'Only in her dreams.'

'But I promised her that I'll always come back. I broke that promise before. I'm never doing that to her again. I have to go back to her, Gran. I have to be with her.'

'That's my boy.'

* * *

Josh opened his eyes and squinted at the dull light in the room. He blinked a couple of times, trying to wake properly. His head felt heavy, and something was on his hand. He glanced down the hospital bed to see Joey's cheek pressed on the top of his fingers. She was sleeping, dribbling on his hand. He then looked over at his elevated leg in plaster and widened his eyes at its existence.

Some people were talking in the near distance. He didn't listen to what they were saying. Their muffled conversation wasn't of interest. He just stared at the blue curtain around one side of his bed, wondering what was on the other side. He then saw the drip attached to his hand and noticed some bruising on his arm.

The voices faded. He glanced back down at Joey. She looked peaceful, but paler than normal. He didn't want to wake her.

A jug of water and a glass were sitting on a cabinet to his side. Just seeing it made him swallow down the dryness in his throat. He really wanted a drink. His head felt fuzzy and his body tight, in need of a good stretch. He wiggled his toes and loosened his jaw.

Joey's face twitched on his hand. He could feel the damp patch where her mouth was.

'Jo,' he whispered. His voice was hoarse and cut into him. She stirred slightly.

He twisted his hand under her cheek so that he could stroke her hair.

She slowly opened her tired eyes and took a moment.

'Hey,' he whispered.

She burrowed her head into his hand for a second, and her tears dripped down between his fingers. She took a steady breath, lifted her head, and got up to lean over his face. 'I knew you'd come back.'

He smiled. 'Promised, didn't I?'

She tenderly kissed him all over his face before gazing back down at him.

There was tiredness in her eyes, along with a faraway look and a whole heap of affection that warmed him completely. He tried to gather his thoughts. 'How long have I been here?'

'This is the second night.'

He already guessed the answer but asked anyway. 'How long have you been here?'

She gave a gentle smile as she softly stroked his cheek. 'Feels like my whole life.'

'You've spent far too long waiting around for me, Joey Walker.'

Some tears escaped her eyes. 'I'll always wait for you, Josh Reynolds.'

He raised one hand to the back of her head and gently pulled her to his mouth. One light brush of her lips against his was all he needed to heal. Just seeing her always cured every part of him. Being with her gave him life. 'Let's go home, Jo.'

She smiled and wiped her damp face. 'Love to.'

He watched her pour him out some water from the jug, taking a deep breath whilst smiling to herself.

'You must be thirsty, Josh.'

'Yeah.'

Her eyes smiled his way. 'Are you hungry as well?'

Well, now that you mention it…

'Jo, I've got this really strange craving for vegetable stew.'

40

Joey

Music in Honeybee Cottage was playing quietly in the kitchen, drowned out by the lively chatter of guests. Josh had wanted a housewarming party, but Joey turned it into a small gathering, saying it was too much for him after only being out of hospital for a week.

Joey brought him some lime-infused water and sat on the sofa between him and Jake.

Jake moved his crutches to the other side, and Anna took them and placed them on the rug.

'Are you tired, Jake?' she asked.

'No. I'm fine. It's a lot quieter in here.'

Joey looked towards the door. 'Yeah, everyone's in the kitchen.' She turned to Josh. 'Maybe this was too soon.'

'We're both okay,' said Josh, looking at his brother. 'And we've got presents.' He smiled over at the stack of moving-in presents sitting by the white contemporary fireplace, which came alight from one press of a remote control and amused Joey every time she pressed the button.

Flowers and gift baskets were bundled together on the other side. All for Josh.

Joey nodded. 'Yes, you've been very spoilt.'

Josh grinned playfully. 'Hey, what can I say, people love me.'

She leaned closer to him, mindful of his injuries, and kissed his cheek. 'I love you.'

She watched his face warm.

'I love you,' he told her.

'Speaking of love,' said Anna. 'As soon as you're up for it, we're going to book a date to get married.'

'Oh yeah, at the registry office in Sandly,' said Josh.

Anna and Jake frowned at him.

'How did you know that?' she asked.

Josh's brow creased. 'I have no idea. I think I dreamt it. I can remember something about Gran. She was baking bread, and she wanted me to kiss a baby for her.'

'Whose baby?' asked Joey.

Josh sipped his water and gave a slight shrug. 'I don't know. No one's got a baby.'

Anna shifted her weight onto her other hip. 'Erm, well…'

All eyes were on her.

'Anna?' questioned Jake.

Anna started twiddling her fingers. 'I did one of those stick tests, and it came up positive, but I haven't had it confirmed by a doctor yet, because the accident happened, and, well…' She stopped talking, as Jake had pulled her into his arms, squashing her face into his white shirt.

'Oh my God,' whispered Joey.

'We're having a baby?' asked Jake quietly. He pulled Anna off his chest to look at her. 'We're having a baby?'

She nodded. 'I think so. The stick said so, but don't you pull me to your chest again. I know your ribs still hurt.'

Joey watched Jake's hands cup Anna's face. His eyes were glossy and his smile was filled with warmth as he kissed her with such love, she felt her own heart warm. She turned to see Josh smiling. He rolled his bright eyes her way and winked.

Jake pulled away. 'Anna… We need… I need… We're going home. You need to rest, and we're going to see the doctor first thing in the morning.'

Anna giggled and got up to fetch his crutches. 'We only decided to start trying last month. Jake wants a hundred kids, so we thought we'd better get on with it. I wasn't expecting anything to happen this fast though.'

'It's the best news,' said Joey, flapping a hand in front of her face. 'I'm so excited. I'm going to cry.'

'Congratulations,' said Josh. 'Don't worry, we'll keep quiet until you're ready to tell the world.'

Joey stood and helped Anna to help Jake to his feet. His ankle was covered by a thick black padded boot, which the hospital had supplied.

'I want to tell the world now,' said Jake, wincing from the pain in his ribs.

'No,' said Anna, smiling up at him. 'Let's wait till we know for sure.'

Jake gave a slight nod. 'Okay. Just our family, for now.'

Anna's eyes welled up as she looked from Josh to Joey, then back to Jake. She leaned closer to his chest without touching him. 'I have a family now, Jake, all thanks to you.'

He kissed her head. 'And mine has grown because of you. Don't forget that.'

Max trotted into the room and snuffled his nose into the side of Anna's leg.

'And I finally have a dog in my life, thanks to you, Anna,' said Josh, grinning.

Anna wrapped her arms around Jake's arm as she turned to Josh. 'You're going to be on dog duty and baby duty.'

'And best man duty,' said Jake.

Josh's smile widened. 'I'd better hurry up and get better.'

Jake hobbled towards the doorway. 'I'll call you tomorrow after we've seen the doctor.'

Joey clasped her hands together in front of her chest. 'I can't wait.' She followed them out to the hallway, where

Jake attempted to help wrap Anna in her coat and scarf whilst juggling his crutches. 'Now that you're off, I'm going to get rid of everyone else too. Whether Josh admits it or not, he's tired and needs to rest.'

Anna helped Jake with his coat whilst he continued to grin stupidly at her.

Joey announced to the kitchen that Josh was tired and it was time for them to leave.

There were some clinking bottles, a few muffled goodbyes, along with hugs and kisses, and Joey had finally cleared everyone from her home.

She flopped back down next to Josh. 'What a night. I feel exhausted. I'll clear up in the morning.'

Josh wriggled his index finger over to a pile of unopened mail by the presents. 'Bring those over, will you, Jo.'

She heaved herself up and got him the two letters and three boxes. 'You know you've officially moved in somewhere when you start getting mail. Did you know, this morning is the first time the postie has come here. Old Arthur said he didn't even know I'd moved here. You would think he would be up to date with these things. He used to know everything that happened around here.' She glanced down at the post on his lap. 'You don't have to do that now, do you?'

He opened a small box. 'Yeah, I've been waiting for something to arrive.'

She watched him open the brown package. There was A H of London stamped on a dark-blue ring box that was inside. He lifted the lid and turned it around to face her. Her eyes widened at the sapphire ring gleaming up at her.

'Not exactly how I planned it,' he said softly, 'but I'm not wasting any more time.'

'Is that what I think it is?'

'Yep. Joey Walker, you are my first everything, and I want you to be my last everything. We both know that we're going to be together forever anyway, so why not get married? Will you marry me?'

Joey's whole face broke out into a smile. 'A thousand times over.'

He gave her a knowing stare. 'Don't you jump on me. My ribs can't handle it.'

She laughed at him. 'Can I put it on?'

'Well, I was hoping you would.'

She waited for him to remove the ring from the box.

He glanced at her eternity ring. 'Oh, do you want to take that one off first.'

'Nope. That's staying put.'

He grinned and slid the ring on her wedding finger.

Joey held her hand up in front of them. 'I love it, Josh. I feel as though you should have one too.'

He scrunched his nose. 'Sapphires aren't really my style.' He waved her towards him so that he could kiss her. 'But I'll wear your wedding ring, Mrs Reynolds.'

She kissed him gently and nudged his cheek with her nose. 'If you weren't so wounded right now…'

'Yeah, I know.'

Joey sat back. 'Hey, do you think Jake and Anna will be up for a double wedding?'

'We can ask, but is that what you really want?'

She lifted her shoulder to her cheek. 'I always dreamed of having a big fancy wedding with you, but now I don't care. I've always wanted to be your wife. If I could bring someone here right now to marry us, I would.'

His eyes smiled warmly into hers. 'I would too.'

'We could always hire Swan Lake for the reception, or we could just celebrate the day with our close friends and family in The Ugly Duckling.'

'I wouldn't mind having the party in your dad's old barn.'

Joey laughed. 'Oh my God, Josh, that would be brilliant.'

'We can sneak away to the top part and have a roll around in the hay like old times.'

'Well, in that case, we're definitely going to have to wait until you're fully healed.'

'Do you remember our first time together?'

'Hmm, how can I forget.'

Josh grinned. 'Hey, I wasn't that bad.'

Joey giggled. 'You were perfect.'

'We both know that's not true.'

'You've always been perfect to me, Josh Reynolds.'

He gave her a cheeky wink and kissed her wedding finger.

Joey sighed happily. She snuggled down under his arm, slightly away from his ribs, and held his hand. 'I hope Anna is pregnant.'

'She is. Gran knew.'

'Your gran's starting to sound like mine.' She felt his chest move as he huffed out a laugh that caused him to wince.

Josh took a shallow breath as she softly rubbed his arm. 'Look at us, Jo. We're so blessed. We've got everything we want.'

'It took us long enough.'

She felt his lips press down on her head.

'We're home now,' he whispered.

She reached over to the glass coffee table and pressed the button on the black remote that lit the fire. She leaned back carefully. 'That table isn't very child friendly. We'll have to buy something else when our new niece or nephew starts running around.'

'Or when our own kids show up. If that's something you want.'

She snuggled her head into his shoulder. 'That is.' She felt his body shift a touch and his mouth press down on her head.

'You just let me know when you're ready.'

'I'm ready.'

'I love you, Jo.'

'I love you too, Josh. Always have, always will.'

They stared into the flickering flames in the fireplace as the music in the kitchen changed. Elvis started to sing "Can't Help Falling in Love with You".

Joey closed her eyes and smiled as Josh started to softly sing along.

* * *

If you enjoyed this story, why not come back for another visit to Pepper Bay with Nate and Tessie.

Pepper Pot Farm

Tessie Sparrow and Nate Walker have everything a relationship can have, except intimacy. Neither of them want to add it into the mix, for fear of ruining their friendship.

It's not easy for them to stay apart when they are growing so close, and Tessie's secret plan to help save Nate's farm might destroy them forever.

Lightning Source UK Ltd.
Milton Keynes UK
UKHW040815300922
409697UK00002B/303